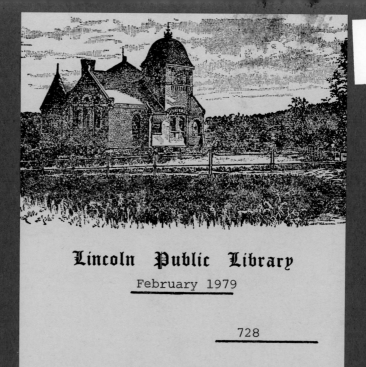

A Treasury of Contemporary Houses

Architectural Record Series

- Apartments, Townhouses and Condominiums, 2/e
- The Architectural Record Book of Vacation Houses, 2/e
- Buildings For Commerce and Industry
- Buildings for the Arts
- Campus Planning and Design
- Great Houses for View Sites, Beach Sites, Sites in the Woods, Meadow Sites, Small Sites, Sloping Sites, Steep Sites, and Flat Sites
- Hospitals and Healthcare Facilities, 2/e
- Houses Architects Design for Themselves
- Houses of the West
- Interior Spaces Designed by Architects
- Office Building Design, 2/e
- Places for People: Hotels, Motels, Restaurants, Bars, Clubs, Community Recreation Facilities, Camps, Parks, Plazas, Playgrounds
- Recycling Buildings: Renovations, Remodelings, Restorations, and Reuses
- Techniques of Successful Practice, 2/e
- A Treasury of Contemporary Houses

Architectural Record Series Books

- Ayers: Specifications for Architecture, Engineering, and Construction
- Feldman: Building Design for Maintainability
- Heery: Time, Cost, and Architecture
- Heimsath: Behavioral Architecture
- Hopf: Designer's Guide to OSHA
- Portman and Barnett: The Architect as Developer
- Redstone: The New Downtowns

A Treasury of Contemporary Houses

by Walter F. Wagner, Jr., AIA

An Architectural Record Book
McGraw-Hill Book Company

New York   Montreal
St. Louis   New Delhi
San Francisco   Panama
Auckland   Paris
Bogotá   São Paulo
Düsseldorf   Singapore
Johannesburg   Sydney
London   Tokyo
Madrid   Toronto
Mexico

Credits

The editors for this book were Jeremy Robinson and Sue Cymes.
The designer was Marianne Gladych.
The production supervisors were Elizabeth Dineen and Frank P. Bellantoni.
The book was set in Optima and Helvetica by Monotype Composition Company, Inc.
Printed and bound by Halliday Lithograph Corporation.

Library of Congress Cataloging in Publication Data

Main entry under title:

A Treasury of contemporary houses.

"An Architectural record book."
1. Architecture, Domestic—United States.
2. Architecture, Modern—20th century—United
States. 3. Dwellings—United States. I. Wagner,
Walter F. II. Architectural record.
NA7208.T73   728.3   78-1448
ISBN 0-07-002330-1
1234567890 HDHD 7654321098

February 1979

Contents

Contents

A Treasury of Contemporary Houses:

What generates the form and "feel" of today's good new custom houses?

A not-too-analytical, surely arguable, idea-exposing study of the "roots" of 54 fine contemporary houses, intended to show the many options in plan, in form, and in character that are available to those who want a house that is truly their own. . . .

Most families buy a house that is built-for-sale. It may be a fine house—but by definition it was designed without reference to the family's special needs and wants and dreams.

There is a bolder breed—those who are unwilling to settle for what the market place offers, and who therefore set out on the process of finding a good architect and building a house which is truly their own—a custom house for them.

Such families have a problem—but it is a wonderful problem.

When they begin to work with their architect, they enter a giant candy store of traditions and new ideas, of alternate forms for their house, and of choices of what the house will "feel like"—its essential character. The most common criticism of contemporary houses is that they are "cold"—but as the houses in this and any other book of good contemporary design shows, that is not really a meaningful indictment. There are families who choose for themselves houses that range far from traditional images of the rose-covered cottage—but that is their choice. In houses that are very much of today, you can evoke all of the warm images of fireplace, brick floors, and cozy nooks, or even of fairy castles—if that is your choice.

The point is: The choice is endless. In this book, we present 54 houses for study. The reader may not find the house that is just right for his or her family;

but that is almost to be expected. No house that has been painstakingly designed and built to meet the needs and wants and dreams of one family *should* meet yours. The point is that in books like this you can search for the design ideas that will, when put together in a different way—by the skill, talent, and training of a good architect—create a house that will meet your wishes.

In an earlier book in this series, we tried to show how houses grow very differently depending on the nature of their sites—why houses for the beach are very different from houses on a mountain stream or in a meadow or on a hillside. In this book, the houses are categorized by the roots of their form—traditional, geometric, even romantic. Houses resist such "pigeon-holing," but perhaps it is one useful technique for helping the reader understand why he or she likes a particular kind of house, and why it is the way it is.

You don't have to agree with the categories—all you have to do is find what you like. Welcome to architecture's wonderful candy store.

WW

Sometimes the form of contemporary houses grows from familiar shapes or from regional traditions centuries old

To illustrate from the houses in this chapter: The Perry House (page 2) uses a form and finishes common to barns everywhere; its roof slope and saltbox shape are familiar, as is the vertical siding of stained boards and the barn doors (hung on standard barn-door hardware) which can be pulled over the lower-level doors and windows to secure the house when the owners are away (it is used only on weekends and vacations). Sensitively, architect Perry used an existing stone fence at a sharp grade change to divide the one- and two-story sections of the house—as was often done in old barns.

For his own house (page 4), architect Lawrence Partridge actually incorporated portions of an old stone barn and its retaining walls into his design, which, while thoroughly contemporary, relates the old to the new by the scale of the new sections and the strong unifying element of the shingle roofs.

For a house in Nantucket (page 6), architect Louis Mackall not only designed-in a lot of hand-crafted details—but built them himself. The unusual bowed roof rafters inevitably conjure up images of the sailing ships that once were the major industry of the area; and everywhere there is a feeling of "something old." Yet, everything is new, for in plan, in the way light is let in, in the way the house is used, it is very much of today.

The next two houses in this chapter are "familiar" because they grow from two different regional traditions: the Barrington, Rhode Island house by Huygens and Tappé (page 10) begins with the big and sheltering shingle roof that dates back to the great shingle mansions built overlooking the harbor at Newport; the other house, on Nantucket Island, gets its familiar feel from the region's ubiquitous cedar shingles and 45-degree roof pitch, though no traditional Cape Cod house would have such a plan or such windows (page 14).

The final two houses, both by architect Charles Moore, are carefully analyzed, compared, and carried back to their roots in a thoughtful essay by RECORD senior editor Mildred Schmertz. Her comparison (page 16) explains, perhaps in a way no description of a single house could, how subtle yet how meaningful the historical precedents and images can be in the design of a house which, in fact, is very contemporary indeed.

1

A Philadelphia lawyer and his family commissioned Lyman Perry to plan this house for their vacation and weekend use. The open-field site slopes sharply to the south and east offering, as it does so, expansive views of the Upper Delaware Valley. An old stone fence, neglected and crumbling, cut east-west across a portion of the hillside. Perry had the fence rebuilt and generated the stepped section of the house by using a portion of the fence as a retaining wall. The expanded saltbox forms are a response to its rural setting, its modest budget, and the requirement to throw off snow in a region of severe winter storms.

The plan is tightly organized around the two intersecting axes of circulation. The lower levels contain living room and kitchen as well as two bedrooms and bath. Bedrooms and a small study occupy the upper level and the upstairs circulation space overlooks the living room (photos below). Both upstairs and down, the circulation spaces are terminated with large glazed openings that provide orienting views to site, fill the interiors with natural light, and are protected by sliding wood panels during inclement weather or when the house is not in use.

The structure is post-and-beam with tongue-and-groove cedar decking. For greater strength and added insulation the stud walls are framed in 2 x 6 members and clad in vertical cedar siding. Floors on the lower level are finished in quarry tile that runs a color range from red-brown to purple.

The Maxey house is a nice example of what can be accomplished on a controlled budget by a designer sensitive to the site and to his client's needs. Not prepossessing, not polemical, not overly fussy, it re-arouses our interest in "timeless" forms and in the simplified lifestyle these forms have long expressed so persuasively.

Architect: Lyman S.A. Perry
  311 North Newton Street Road
  Newton Square, Pennsylvania
Owner: David W. Maxey
Engineers:
  Keast and Hood (structural)
Contractor: Norella Brothers
Photographer: Positive Two Studios

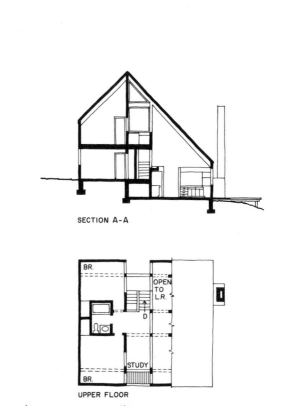

SECTION A-A

UPPER FLOOR

MAIN FLOOR
5

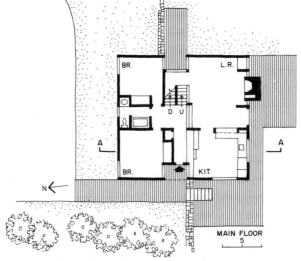

As the interior photos below clearly indicate, the spatial development of the house is vertical with overlooks and see-throughs used to emphasize this verticality. Not shown in plan is a detached, two-car garage with work shed.

2

In designing and building for his own family, architect Lawrence Partridge had no original intention of buying an existing building to remodel as a home, but an old New England barn with its beautiful glacial stone foundation and walls had a compelling appeal. Together with program and site, the scale and character of the parts of the 1890 structure which were saved established the scale and character of the design.

The stepped slope of the site suggested the roof relationships of the three new sections which were added to the existing structure (the rest of the barn was demolished). Thus, the fragmented appearance of the house was in part planned to reduce the scale of these walls. In the photo of the rear of the house, right, the old building can be seen on the right. The various wings contain, from the left of the photo, dining room; kitchen and a bedroom; stairhall; and, in the old building, family room on the lower level, with two bedrooms and bath located on the second floor and a workroom office on the third. An arrangement of fixed insulating glass window, bifolding storage cabinet, wood door ventilator and screen was designed for use throughout the house, further contributing to the strong exterior rhythm and scale. Roughsawn fir shiplap siding painted white and a white cedar shingle roof respect a New England vernacular and offset the original walls. Contrasting interior materials include natural wool carpeting for living areas, natural red oak trim and drywall, painted white, except where glacial stone walls are left exposed.

ARCHITECT'S OWN HOUSE, Weston, Massachusetts. Owner and architect: *Lawrence Partridge*; engineers: *Arthur Choo (structural)*; *Terenzio Genovesi (heating and ventilation)*; contractor: *Costa Limberakis*.

The living room (photo above) reaches a dramatic 23-foot height. The photo is taken from an upper-bedroom opening designed to provide added ventilation for the living and dining rooms. At right is the master bedroom whose curved windows are openings of the original wall.

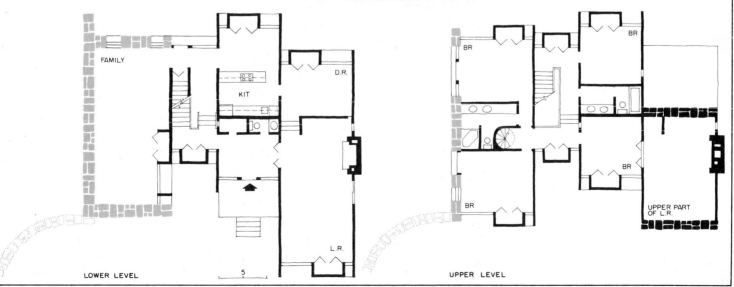

FAMILY

KIT

D.R.

L.R.

LOWER LEVEL

5

BR

BR

BR

BR

BR

UPPER PART OF L.R.

UPPER LEVEL

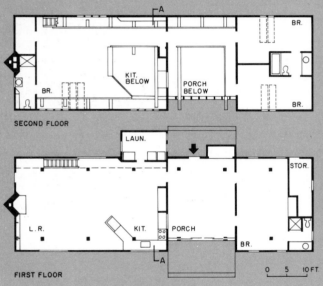

SECOND FLOOR

LAUN.

L.R.   KIT.   PORCH

STOR.

BR.

FIRST FLOOR

0   5   10 FT.

Given the client's request for heavy timber framing, the architect suggested this architectural anachronism be placed in quotes, so to speak. Prominently exhibited, the oak 10 x 10s actually support the second floor, but the exterior walls of the house are conventional framing, with the rafters—sawn from 3x12s—two feet on center, tied in pairs by tension rods. The house is shingled in white cedar, and interior flooring is tongue-and-groove fir.

3

''We can extrude almost anything now,'' says architect Louis Mackall. ''People are surrounded by objects, which are there only because people can afford them. But eventually they realize that their whole environment is foreign to them, that they have no personal attachment to anything in it. That's why so many people are turning to handcraft . . . making things for themselves, or having things made for them.''

Mackall built many of the parts of the Wierdsma house himself in his Connecticut shop—the skylights, cabinets, doors and screen doors, the stairs—everything that could be conveniently carried in a moving van. ''I could go on forever making stuff for this house,'' he says as he eases out one or two of the drawers in the kitchen. Feeling a slight hesitation in the glide, he goes out to find his plane.

The house crosses the upland at the head of a long marsh stretching out of Pulpis Bay across from the town of Nantucket. With its silvery bowed roof, it resembles a weathered log, ax-cut once in the center for a tall, interior porch, and notched toward the ends for skylights.

Beneath the master bedroom, upper right, a low ceiling slides over the giant beams, making a more intimate family space. Whaling artifacts hang on the fir columns and beams. In front of the tall fireplace, the children can hash out a game of Monopoly. ''I hope all this wood, this handcraft, will be an important part of these kids' childhood and recollections,'' Mackall says.''I hope it makes a difference.''

Architect: Louis Mackall
  1079 Rt. 80 RD2
  Guilford, Connecticut
Owners: Mr. and Mrs. John Wierdsma
Location: Nantucket, Massachusetts
Contractor: Ron DaSilva
Photographer: Robert Perron

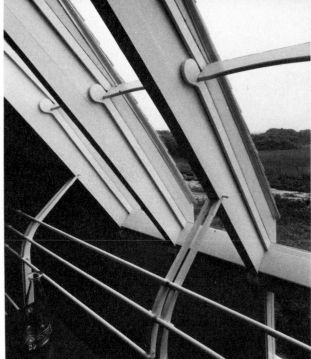

The ten-by-ten oak network pierces the walls, enhancing the sense of wood enclosure in the two-story kitchen, left, which is finished in teak: teak-faced counters and drawers with brass inlay on either side of the range. A brass oval inlaid in the counter is provided for setting down hot skillets. The round table for six is in teak segments, with a segmented center rotating section, and a brass inlay in its center. A barber's chair pedestal supports the table, allowing height variation to accommodate adults or the four younger Wierdsmas. The eye floats up to the balcony, railed in by white electrical conduit that serves also to light the areas above and below with bare-reflector floods. The skylight, photo upper left, follows the bowed roof with sheets of glass stepping down; the joints are ship-lapped. Each tread of the living room stair-ladder, above, is a version of the inverted king-post truss in tension. The child's ladder, upper right, was designed by the architect and built by the owner, John Wierdsma. Three oak crosspieces stiffen the pine doors, right, and the middle crosspiece, shown, includes hardware. To open, one pulls on the wood tongue.

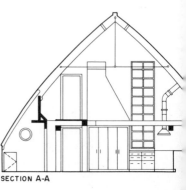

SECTION A-A

Julius Shulman photos

4

Seen from Narragansett Bay, (above), this elegant house seems to have been around as long as any of its late nineteenth-century neighbors. Huygens and Tappé have used the cedar-clad roof volumes with knife-edged eaves to capture a special regional quality and to anchor the relatively small house securely to its open site.

Yet the plan reveals a relaxed openness that can only be found in houses of our time. Recognizing that few will arrive except by automobile, the architects have used the entrance gallery to connect garage to house and to create a court protected from offshore winds.

Occupied most of the time by only two people, the house is complete on one floor. Upstairs, two bedrooms which share a bath and a small sitting area are provided for visits of children who no longer live at home. A dining table designed by the architects opens to accommodate all of them.

The materials are limited, but rich. Walls on the exterior are white-painted boards and battens, on the interior, white plaster. Floors in the entrance gallery, kitchen and dining room are Welsh quarry tile, carpet elsewhere. To mitigate mid-day glare from the bay, all ceilings are wood: matte-finished birch

paneling with battens. Given the quietly eclectic furnishings, the effect is again reminiscent of a turn-of-the century house at the shore. On the approach facade (overpage), rain-washed white paint from a massive brick chimney has stained the cedar shingles, a patina which helps the house seem mature.

Architects: REMMERT HUYGENS and ANTHONY TAPPÉ of Huygens and Tappé, Inc., Terry A. Cracknell, job captain. *Location:* Barrington, Rhode Island. *Engineers:* Souza and True (structural), William R. Ginns (mechanical), Lottero and Mason Associates, Inc. (electrical). *Contractor:* E. J. Sevigny Construction Co.

The skylight (above) not only illuminates the entry hall, but lightens the profile of what might otherwise have been a forbiddingly heavy roof. Wide overhangs and the dark ceiling help minimize glare in the living room (right).

The stairway to the second floor bedrooms (right) and the upstairs sitting area are lit by corner dormers on the garden side (above) and the entry side (below) of the roof which connects the house and garage.

Nick Wheeler photos

5

This vacation house was designed for a three-generation family to spend holidays together in. Grandparents, parents and children use the house simultaneously and require as much privacy as possible. The plan permits the parents and children to share the lower level with its own private entry, two master bedrooms and a bunkroom for the children. The grandparents share a bedroom, bath and study on the upper level. The middle level is devoted to shared living, dining, and kitchen.

The design had to take into account views of the Atlantic Ocean to the east and Nantucket Harbor to the west. In keeping with the traditional architecture of Nantucket, examples of which border the house on both sides (top photo this page), roof planes were pitched at 45 degrees and the entire house was clad in cedar shingles. To take advantage of both spectacular views, the living level and terraces were placed on the second floor.

To circumvent the difficulties of island construction, the house was designed in modular panels and pre-fabricated elsewhere.

PRIVATE RESIDENCE, Nantucket Island, Massachusetts. Owners: *Mr. and Mrs. Preston C. Carnes.* Architects: *Architectural Resources Cambridge, Inc.* Engineers: *Weidemann Brown, Inc.* (structural). Contractor: *Spacemaker, Inc.*

UPPER LEVEL

MIDDLE LEVEL

LOWER LEVEL

TWO HOUSES BY CHARLES MOORE

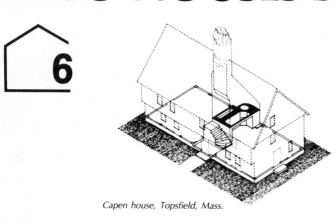

Capen house, Topsfield, Mass.

Stratford Hall, Westmoreland County, Va.

Axonometric drawings by
William Turnbull from The Place of Houses by Charles Moore,
Gerald Allen and Donlyn Lyndon

Robert Motherwell, the abstract expressionist painter, once wrote: "Every intelligent painter carries the whole culture of modern painting in his head. It is his real subject, of which everything he paints is both an homage and a *critique,* and everything he says a gloss." Charles Moore carries the whole culture of architecture in his head. His art lies in his power over the art of the past, his ability to bring forth out of memory timeless forms to convey unchanging human feelings. He does it differently from the other historicizing architects, best represented perhaps by Robert Stern, who in a single house will skillfully juxtapose attached bits and pieces from many cultures—a molding over a door inspired by Sir Edwin Lutyens, or a fireplace mysteriously derived from George Howe. Moore's houses, like Stern's, are complicated in composition and imagery and crowded with meanings, yet they seem to emerge from memory whole—a house is a church, a barn, a farmhouse, an early settler's house in Massachusetts or an antebellum mansion in Virginia, not a collage of assorted references. Moore creates images that recall buildings one was once moved by. And one is stirred again.

The two Moore houses to be contrasted were designed for clients with dissimilar needs. The larger of the two (above right) is located in a meadow of a beautiful farm. It has approximately 11,000 square feet of space on two levels and is for a family of four. The husband, who is blind, hoped that the house would do more than enhance the visual world of his wife and two small sons—a relatively easy task for a good architect. In addition, he wished his new house to speak to his remaining senses—principally those of smell and touch, not only to give him pleasure but to orient him within the spaces of the house. The little Swan house (above left) built on a small piece of land with a view of Long Island Sound is for a woman who entertains frequently but who also enjoys being alone. Thus different in scale and function, each house evokes its owner's beliefs, needs, fantasies and feelings in forms shaped by Moore's mastery of style.

The Swan house suggests a humble rural farm building of no particular time or place

The Swan house is the first small house Moore has designed in several years. It is an important addition to his body of work since he designs small houses particularly well—even better, some believe, than he does big houses. Moore believes that the typical house architect of today doesn't know how to do "big houses," but only "small houses" of small and large sizes. Such an architect will devise an open plan of the type originally conceived to allow for the best multi-use of a small house's limited space, as in the Swan house, and scale it up to whatever dimensions his client can afford. Moore's large houses, in contrast, are an aggregation of self-contained ample rooms like big houses always were in the past.

Simone Swan is an artist, and a friend and patron of artists, and is the mother of two grown children. Charles Moore became her architect after the death of her first choice, Louis Kahn, who had not yet begun to design her house when he died. Before his death he had encouraged her in her wish to buy and tear down an old farm building to obtain a stockpile of hand-hewn joists, flooring and beams and these, as arranged by Moore, are Kahn's legacy to the house.

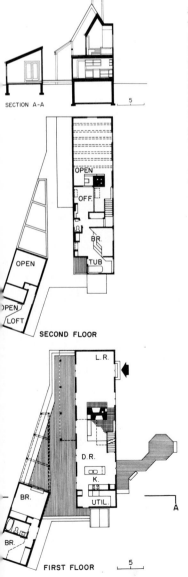

SECTION A-A

SECOND FLOOR

FIRST FLOOR

When she met Charles Moore at a dinner party, Simone didn't know that he was a "Post Modern Movement Radical Eclectic," but she liked him nonetheless and felt intuitively that he was the right architect for her. He began, like a psychoanalyst, to help her discover and express her own inner fantasies and dreams as well as her everyday needs. She had sought a subtle variety of experiences in her house to be. In her words she wanted: "Bathing while looking at the trees, sitting in the winter sun protected from winds, a 'secret' tower terrace. . . ." Moore's first design, a hipped-roof square with a projecting wing met all these specifications and more, but it didn't seem right to her. She flew with the model neatly tucked under her plane seat to Findhorn in Northern Scotland, a spiritual community devoted in part to ecological concerns. Her purpose was to show it to her son Eric, then in his early twenties, who while living at Findhorn was researching the applications of such energy-saving alternative technologies as solar heating and waste recycling. Mother and son agreed that the house, unfortunately, was "not Zen, not severe, not pared to the bone." It was too cozy, rather worldly, a bit "suburban classy" they thought. So Moore and his collaborator Mark Simon returned to the drafting board and model shop armed with a better knowledge of Simone's esthetic, spiritual and practical aspirations. The house became elongated, the roof pitched 60 degrees toward the sun to eventually carry solar collectors. A *clivus multrum* was discussed, but rejected, as

a not yet practical way to produce fertilizer for the vegetable garden. The house lost its suburban slickness and became uncompromisingly rural in its expression, with economical, straightforward carpenter-like finishes and details, including wide trim.

The house image Moore conceived for Simone is perceived by herself and others in a number of different ways, although all these perceptions have a common theme, the simplicity and friendliness of the little building. For Simone it is like an old country chapel, for others it suggests a humble rural farmhouse of no particular time or place. Simone has had visitors of widely differing cultures, each of whom has been reminded of the modest farm buildings of his own country. For Mark Simon it is "friendly, a gingerbread house without the frosting."

It is also the Capen house of 1683 (opposite), in the way its rooms are arranged around a central chimney for warmth in winter, and the manner in which one circulates through it from one room to the next in the absence of a hall. And like the Capen house the cooking utensils are right in one of the main rooms, and the stair wraps around the chimney.

This room (overleaf) with its stair and chimney corner and dining table and its kitchen, which is like no other kitchen, is the heart of the house. The plan brings the cook and her guests together in the friendliest way. Moore has very cleverly placed a mirror at the back of the kitchen counter, which reflects the fire and the guests to allow Simone to communicate with them

and to allow diners with their backs to the fire to see it. Mirrors are also used to box in all the skylights to make the most of the light from them and to give a mysterious and magical quality to these openings.

The house has been designed so that only the heart of the house need be heated in winter. Large one-foot-thick foam cushions were designed by Moore and Mark Simon to serve as living room furniture in the summer, but also to stack up, sealing the two large openings between the cooking-dining area and the living area during the winter. By this means, the living room can be left unheated and the house remains well insulated, saving considerable energy and cost. Heat circulating fireplaces are used along with high return air registers for an oil-fired hot air heating system to recirculate the heat given off by the fireplaces.

THE SWAN HOUSE, Long Island, N.Y. Owner: *Simone Swan.* Architects: *Charles W. Moore Associates (now Moore Grover Harper, P.C.)—project manager: Mark Simon.* General contractor: *Eastwind Homes, Inc.*

Simone's bed is a stepped platform with cedar-lined drawers below. She likes the idea of sleeping, bathing and dressing in the same room so her bedroom accommodates an old clawfooted bathtub next to a window with a view of Long Island Sound. The narrow, high interior of the house is divided by a double fireplace, which separates the living room (opposite page) from the kitchen and dining areas (right top and bottom). The wood from an old barn is used to great advantage as collar ties and trusses in the two-story living room, and on the lower dining and kitchen ceiling.

The large house shown in juxtaposition to the little Swan house was designed for clients who wish to remain anonymous. The man, facing blindness, bought a lovely farm while he could still see. Subsequently, when he and his wife began to interview architects, his loss of vision was almost total. Several of the architects with whom they spoke were understandably reluctant to undertake the design of a house that one of the clients would never see. Moore, however, was drawn to the couple by their spiritual resources. He found himself in great sympathy with the husband's ability to draw strength from his family life, his wish to help create a beautiful house for his wife and two small boys and his desire to have his own remaining senses fulfilled by his surroundings.

The house went through many revisions generally in the direction of becoming less complicated. Moore and his fellow architect, Richard Oliver, made several models and in addition devised a way to cast the plans in braille. The vacuum-forming process was used to produce pearly white plastic sheets, beautiful in themselves, embodying the imprint of the house plans in relief. The blind client, by moving his fingers over their surfaces was able to understand how the circulation would flow and the rooms interrelate.

The house has many textures, smells and breezes that tell the husband where he is. The air moving through the house is a signal to him— he knows from which direction it is coming by the scents it carries,

whether from the lawn or a particular grove of trees; from the garden or one or the other of the two indoor conservatories known respectively as the Orangerie and the Jungle Garden, which form the main foyer and hall. This hall twists and turns and widens and narrows like an ancient street, and is paved in tile which by its resonance tells the client he is not in the living room or dining room which have their rugs centered on hardwood floors. The sound of trickling water in a fountain located in the Jungle Garden (page 22) is another orienting element as is the texture of the stone walls, which are the boundaries of the living room, the dining room and the study. Snaking through this main hall, becoming a bannister at the stair and ending in the second floor hall is a beautiful wooden guide rail shaped in section to match exactly the dimensions of a handrail the client discovered in an airport which felt right to him.

More subtly, the client can tell where he is by means of what he calls ambient sound which communicates to him the size and dimensions of the room he is in. For this reason, among others, he wished the rooms of his house to be discrete and contained, rather than flowing into one another—a desire that fitted neatly with Moore's ideas about what spaces should be like in large houses.

The Orangerie and the Jungle Garden are a quotation from the great square room centered between the two pavilions at Stratford Hall. Although asymmetrical, Moore's derivation is similar to the 18th century space in that it forms the basis for ar-

ranging everything else. It is the symbolic as well as the actual circulation space.

Moore likes to please the knowing by enriching the significance of a quotation from tradition by deliberately altering it, thus intriguing them by the way he has made it resemble, yet not resemble, the original. Stratford Hall, his model and metaphor for this large house, has two pavilions connected by the aforementioned great square room each with a cluster of four chimneys. Moore's house is basically a three pavilion arrangement, each with a cluster of chimneys and cupolas used as ventilators. In contrast to Stratford Hall, however, Moore's ensemble is so complex and deflected in form that the pavilions emerge as the trace of an idea rather than as discrete forms. Moore's final design expresses the fact that for his clients, the Stratford metaphor is too classic, too formal, too rigid. One suspects that Moore began with Stratford as a way to find his own voice, and that once again he has.

The couple entertain frequently and sometimes formally, but their everyday life is informal and the wife does her own housework. For this reason, the plan combines spaces in which life can be lived with ceremony as in the elegant living room, symmetrical in plan but not section, or the dining room with its tall bay windows (page 21), or with unbuttoned ease in the family kitchen, den and pool.

Like Simone Swan, these clients became energy-conscious during the design process, with the result that the house has been zoned in such a way

that rooms not in use are not heated. The house is well insulated and cross ventilated with a fan in the highest cupola to draw the hot air up and out. The bedrooms, guest room, kitchen, and dining room can be air conditioned on the hottest days, but generally air conditioning is not used because of the owner's dependence upon his sense of smell.

A HOUSE NEAR NEW YORK. Architects: *Charles W. Moore with Richard B. Oliver.* Consultants: *Spiegel & Zamecnik* (structural); *Everett Barber* (mechanical); *Richard C. Peters* (lighting); *Tina Beebe* (colors).

The house has a central conservatory—which is also the main circulation element—(below and overleaf) and which changes direction several times as it meanders through what is unmistakably a Moore house. All the elements are there: the cheerful collage of building materials—tile floors, stone walls, other walls of wood siding with trim—and the intriguing complications—steps, orange trees and other plants, skylights, a bridge and a fountain, two round wooden columns with curious brackets and the occasional interior panel with a window. In contrast, the rooms this hall interconnects are surprisingly formal and elegant.

The bedrooms of the large house are shaped by their roofs

The guest bedroom (left) has a carpet of painted flowers. The bedroom of one of the sons is at the highest point of the house where the old-fashioned double-hung windows are stepped upward toward a cluster of chimneys and cupolas. The master bedroom (below right) is under a roof supported by a diagonal truss whose horizontal member becomes a dragon as its tensile stresses are continued by cable.

In contrast, more and more of today's houses are being shaped by the new need and desire to save energy

As fuel becomes increasingly scarce and expensive, more and more architects are experiencing with ways to reduce the need for energy—and more and more clients are accepting their ideas. The five houses in this chapter explore both passive (purely design) techniques and active (solar collector) methods of energy conservation. Since the techniques and technology of such houses are not yet thoroughly understood, they must be considered experimental, but they all seem to be working and they surely are forerunners of many more.

The house overleaf was designed and built on speculation by a young architecture graduate from Yale, and uses a principle that has been understood since the days of the cavemen: caves are warm in the winter and cool in the summer.

The next house, by architect John Johansen, makes use of the "green house" principle—taking advantage of winter sun to heat the major central space of the house through insulating glass that, in summer, is shaded by the trees.

The final three houses explore various techniques of solar collection—all effective, all at least reasonable in cost, and all in houses far from the Sun belt where such use of the sun's rays is relatively easy. They also explore the difficult design problem of integrating solar collectors into the mass of the house—and solve it well.

On property he already owned in Lyme, New Hampshire, designer Don Metz built this sod-roofed house for sale. "I was bothered," says Metz, who holds a Masters degree in architecture from Yale, "by the prospect of anything other than the low-profile, 'anti-building' solution I knew the site demanded, so I borrowed and built on spec. The present owners—Mr. and Mrs. Oliver Winston—were interested before it was completed, made a few minor changes, and that was that."

The finished house is built into a mountainside and embraces a panoramic, 50-mile view to the south. Metz has drawn the earth back down over the roof to a depth of 16 inches. Wildflowers and grasses have already taken root and a stand of nearby maples is slowly spreading to the rooftop. Its designer hopes the house will gradually disappear among the things that grow around it.

Metz reports that in winter solar gain is sufficient on sunny days to keep the temperatures in the house up to 70°F while outside temperatures are as low as zero. In summer, when the thermal process is reversed, the insulating mantle of earth keeps the house pleasantly cool.

The projections through the sod roof are functional and, though some readers may feel that they compromise the purity of the design parti, it is hard to see how to do without light scoops or roof vents in a plan with such a long "blind" perimeter. As c[...] structed, the dining area is suffused w[...] natural light and free of unwelcome gl[...] The living room opens south across a [...] race and small pool to a broad vista [...] mountain and valley.

Exterior walls are concrete bl[...] spanned on 18-inch centers by 6- by 10 [...] pine beams. Floors are oak strips na[...] over sleepers. The roof is built-up (see [...] tail, opposite page) and finished with a [...] apet of vertical boards.

WINSTON HOUSE, Lyme, New Hampshire. [...] signer and contractor: *Don Metz.* Structural e[...] neers: *Spiegel & Zamecnik, Inc.* Landscape [...] chitect: *Dan Kiley.* Built-ins: *William Porter,*

Robert Perron photos

COPPER GRAVEL STOP

1'-6"

EARTH FILL

6" x 10"

8 WF 17

1" x 6"

6" x 10"
PLASTERED

SECTION THROUGH GARAGE

GARAGE

ST.

STUDY   D.R.   K

BR.   MUSIC   L.R.   BR.

N

5

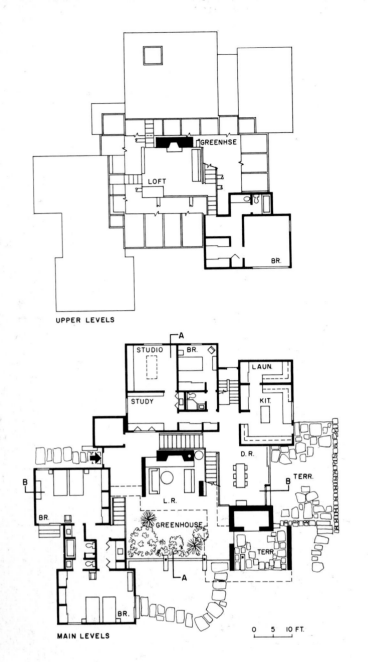

GREENHSE

LOFT

UPPER LEVELS

STUDIO BR.

STUDY

LAUN.

KIT.

D.R.

TERR.

L.R.

BR.

GREENHOUSE

TERR.

BR.

MAIN LEVELS

0 5 10 FT.

2

The inventive thread that runs so persistently through John Johansen's work is evident in this Connecticut house both in its planning and in its detail. The owner has a professional interest in plants, including exotic species, so the house was conceived as a tall greenhouse, flanked on three sides by simple wood enclosures that contain bedrooms, kitchen, laundry, studio and garage. Outdoor decks, on top of two of these enclosures, are an added amenity. Uniting all of these—and giving the exteriors whatever formal properties they may be said to have—is a remarkable, 30-foot-high volume, framed in actual greenhouse sections, that contains living and dining platforms and, underneath, an intimate, grotto-like den with stone fireplace and earthen floor.

An elaborate and winding system of stairs connects the five separate levels within the greenhouse. Constructed of steel tube stringers and pipe handrails, both painted bright red, the stair system energizes the interiors and intensifies their already kinetic qualities.

A second, even more linear design element is the system of ex-posed ductwork. Hung from the ceiling of the den, these polished sheet metal tubes branch out in all directions, delivering tempered air through adjustable outlets to people and plants in any part of the space. This kind of ductwork, until recently regarded as architectural slang within the more formal vocabulary of design, is here given legitimacy and elegance.

The glazed walls are double thick for insulation and fitted with operable metal blinds to control the light. But even with these controls, humidity and temperature are balanced as much for plants as for people in a frank acknowledgement of their environmental interdependency.

And this is not the only design ambiguity. Looking out through rows of potted plants toward the lovely wooded site, the distinction between what is inside and what is not becomes pleasantly blurred—only to be resolved, then blurred again, by each successive change of vantage.

Architect: John Johansen
   401 East 37th Street
   New York, New York 10016
Private residence
Location: Central Connecticut
Engineers: KBNA/B Associates (structural)
   John Altieri (mechanical)
Interior designer:
   Maria Radoslovich
Landscape architect: Multi-service
Contractor: Gilligan Brothers
Photographer: Norman McGrath

PRIVATE RESIDENCE BY JOHN JOHANSEN

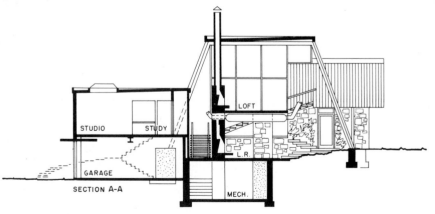

SECTION A-A

(labels in section drawing: STUDIO, STUDY, GARAGE, LOFT, L.R., MECH.)

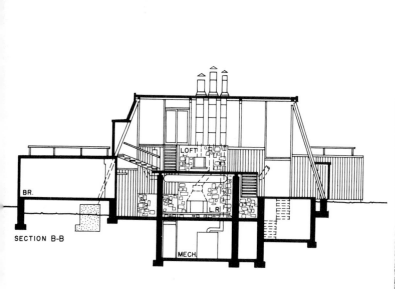

SECTION B-B

BR.

LOFT

L.R.

MECH.

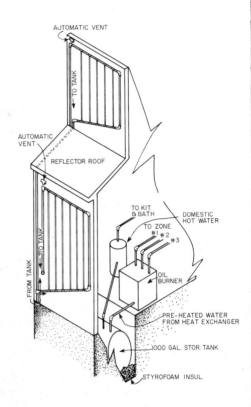

Robert Perron photos

SOLAR HOUSES

FOR THREE ALL-WEATHER SITES IN THE NORTHEAST

Solar heating, as a concept, has been around a long, long time. But because solar energy, when collected at the earth's surface, is both dilute and intermittent, its architectural application, until recently, has been sharply limited. Today, however, with increasing environmental concern, with more intensive research, with technical improvements and, most important, with the soaring costs and uncertain availability of fossil fuels, architects and their clients are looking at solar heating with new interest.

Here are three houses that reflect this growing concern. Each is strikingly different in program, form and adaptation for solar use. And none are located under the cloudless skies of Arizona or New Mexico. The first (photo above) is a weekend house in the mountains of Vermont. The second is a year-round built-for-sale house north of New York City. The third is a passive application in a suburban Princeton house. All are somewhat intuitive in design and all make comprehensive use of siting, materials, and a variety of design skills to minimize their reliance on backup heating. What they represent, as a group, are the kinds of solutions that the profession must be prepared to provide on this increasingly crowded, resource-depleted planet.

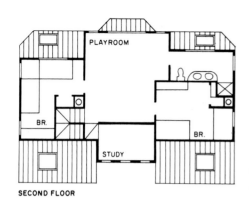

PLAYROOM

BR.

BR.

STUDY

SECOND FLOOR

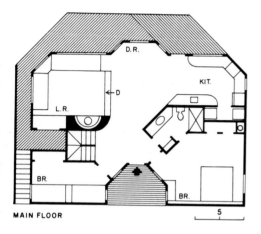

D.R.

KIT.

L.R.

D

BR.

BR.

MAIN FLOOR

5

ON A VERMONT MOUNTAIN, AN INTEGRAL SYSTEM FOR SOLAR COLLECTION, STORAGE AND TRANSFER

Okemo Mountain, in Ludlow, Vermont, has an elevation of 3700 feet, winter temperatures that sometimes do not rise above 15°F for periods as long as 21 days, and a winter sunshine factor in the range of 40-45 per cent. These chilling conditions make the mountain a magnet for weekend skiers, like the owners of this house, but sorely challenge the solar designer. Architects Ric Weinshenk and Martha Poole of *Sunshine Design* accepted the challenge and designed this strong-massed, 3000-square-foot weekend house in a birch grove on this gently sloping, windswept site.

The solar collection system is integral to the design rather than imposed on it. Backed by a layer of insulating foam, the system is a grid of ¾-inch copper pipe and ⅜-inch refrigeration tubing shielded on the outside by two ¹⁄₁₆-inch thicknesses of fiberglass with a ¾-inch airspace between. The visual result is the series of opaque panels that are the predominant feature of the south elevation. The whole collector surface is about 1000 square feet (or ⅓ the floor area of the house) and it faces just east of due south to take advantage of the morning sun. Water, passing through the col-

lector, is heated then returned to a 1000 gallon storage tank where it awaits circulation to the boiler by way of the heat exchanger.

Because the principal view is to the north, more than the minimum number of openings occur on this elevation, but all windows are double glazed and fitted with custom-designed, almost airtight insulating curtains that can be drawn to trap heat at night or when the house is not in use. This window treatment, combined with six inches of insulation in the stud walls and 12 inches at the roof, produces an R factor of ± 20 for walls and 30 for roof.

Additional heat is provided by a fireplace—not just by radiation but by a heavy heating coil that serves as an andiron and keeps a flow of heated water going to the storage tank whenever the fireplace is in use.

Beyond its mechanical invention, this Vermont house is spatially lively and fresh in its graphic images.

PRIVATE RESIDENCE, Ludlow, Vermont. Architects and builders: *Sunshine Design*—Ric Weinshenk, partner-in-charge.

Robert Perron photos

FLAT-PLATE COLLECTORS MEET AT LEAST HALF THE DEMAND FOR HEAT IN A NEW YORK HOUSE

This house, on a site 30 miles north of New York City, is interesting because it indicates how a conventional developer's plan can be remassed and adapted for solar heating. The need to appeal to a broad market of potential buyers led to a program that includes four bedrooms, separate living and dining rooms, family room and two-and-a-half baths. This program produced about 2400 square feet plus basement and a two-car garage.

The decision to use solar collectors, together with the sloping site, suggested to architects Raymond, Rado, Caddy & Bonington a compact volume and a stacking of elements. Six inches of glass fiber insulation fill the wall cavities and 12 inches are applied at the ceiling of the second floor and at the first floor under the deck. This heavy insulation, coupled with a modest use of glass, keeps heat loss to about 100,000 Btus per hour—this in a region with an average winter temperature of 42°F and approximately 4900 degree days.

The deeply-sloping roof faces just west of due south and is inclined at 50 degrees—an angle assumed to be optimal for solar collection at this latitude. This roof is fitted with a system of flat-plate aluminum collectors with a surface area equal to nearly one-half the square footage of floor space to be heated. The liquid medium (water treated with an antifreeze solution) is picked up in manifold pipes between the collectors, then conveyed to a heat exchanger in the basement. Here the heat is transferred to a conventional forced-air distribution system before being recirculated to the collector system on the roof. To protect against a protracted period of overcast or rainy weather, a standby oil-fired heater trips on automatically when the water temperature in the storage tank has dropped below usable levels for space heating. Both solar and conventionally generated heat are of course distributed by the same system of ducts.

Domestic hot water demands are also met by a solar system and backed up by an electric heater. The two backup systems might theoretically have been unified but, in this instance, discrete systems were more economical.

Apart from the solar-heating collectors, their mechanical adjuncts, and the heavier level of insulation, the construction and selection of finishes is typical of the better quality built-for-sale housing in this region. The roof is finished in asphalt shingles, the walls are clad in textured plywood siding except at the foundation, where ribbed concrete blocks were used. The site had no special treatment except the removal of a few close-in trees that otherwise would have filtered the sunlight before it reached the collectors.

HOUSE in New Castle, New York. Architects: *Raymond, Rado, Caddy & Bonington;* structural engineers: *Weidlinger Associates;* solar energy collection system: *General Energy Devices, Inc.;* builders; *John Reventas and Carlo Ventimiglia.*

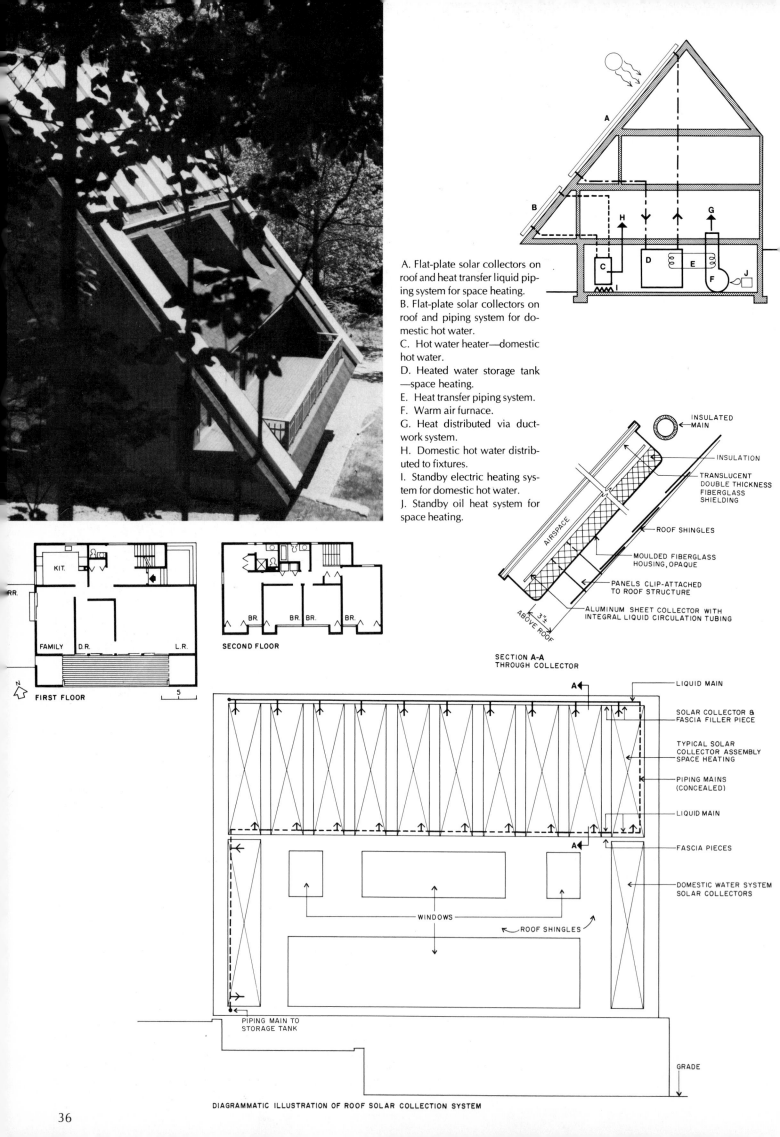

A. Flat-plate solar collectors on roof and heat transfer liquid piping system for space heating.
B. Flat-plate solar collectors on roof and piping system for domestic hot water.
C. Hot water heater—domestic hot water.
D. Heated water storage tank —space heating.
E. Heat transfer piping system.
F. Warm air furnace.
G. Heat distributed via ductwork system.
H. Domestic hot water distributed to fixtures.
I. Standby electric heating system for domestic hot water.
J. Standby oil heat system for space heating.

KIT.

FAMILY   D.R.   L.R.

FIRST FLOOR

SECOND FLOOR

BR.   BR. BR.   BR.

N

5

INSULATED MAIN
INSULATION
TRANSLUCENT DOUBLE THICKNESS FIBERGLASS SHIELDING
ROOF SHINGLES
MOULDED FIBERGLASS HOUSING, OPAQUE
PANELS CLIP-ATTACHED TO ROOF STRUCTURE
ALUMINUM SHEET COLLECTOR WITH INTEGRAL LIQUID CIRCULATION TUBING
AIRSPACE
3¼ ABOVE ROOF

SECTION A-A THROUGH COLLECTOR

LIQUID MAIN
SOLAR COLLECTOR & FASCIA FILLER PIECE
TYPICAL SOLAR COLLECTOR ASSEMBLY SPACE HEATING
PIPING MAINS (CONCEALED)
LIQUID MAIN
FASCIA PIECES
DOMESTIC WATER SYSTEM SOLAR COLLECTORS
WINDOWS
ROOF SHINGLES
PIPING MAIN TO STORAGE TANK
GRADE

DIAGRAMMATIC ILLUSTRATION OF ROOF SOLAR COLLECTION SYSTEM

HEAT RADIATED FROM A HUGE CONCRETE WALL WARMS THE OWNERS OF THIS PRINCETON HOUSE

The Kelbaugh house is a 2100-square-foot, year-round residence in suburban Princeton, a community with a 40 degree north latitude, a climate that typically includes 5100 heating degree days, and a 50-55 per cent sunshine factor during the winter.

By obtaining a zoning variance, the Kelbaughs were able to push the house to the northern boundary of their 60- by 100-foot lot, thus clearing the pattern of shadows cast by neighboring houses and at the same time, giving the lot an ample outdoor space instead of the usual mishmash of shallow yards.

The key to the solar capabilities of the design is the massive concrete wall, an adaptation of the "Trombe wall" (see section drawing) set back six inches from the glass curtain wall that faces south. The 600-square-foot concrete surface absorbs and stores heat from the sun and radiates it continually into living spaces that are nearly uninterrupted spatially both upstairs and down. Back-up space heating has been provided by a gas-fired, hot air system, independent of the house's solar capabilities, but with ductwork cast into the concrete wall.

During its first winter (a mild one with about 4500 degree days), the Kelbaugh house performed well. With the thermostat for the back-up system set in the 60-64°F range (58°F at night), only 338 cubic feet of natural gas was consumed. This represented a saving of nearly 75 per cent when compared with the estimated 1220 cubic feet of gas that would have been required to maintain a 65°F daytime temperature by conventional heating. And these savings came at little sacrifice to comfort. The temperatures inside were allowed to swing 3-6 degrees during the 24-hour cycle to allow the concrete wall to collect and discharge its heat. Auxiliary 250-watt infrared heaters were installed in the bathroom but seldom needed and the fireplace was used several times a week for localized comfort.

Insulation, of course, is critical. Kelbaugh provided an average 4-inch wall insulation of cellulosic fiber (recycled newspaper) and a 9½-inch roof insulation that achieved an R factor of 40. In addition, he used a one-inch thickness of polystyrene (two inches would have been better, he reports) on the perimeter foundation wall to a depth of two feet. The re-

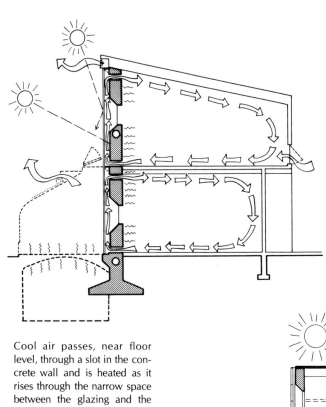

Cool air passes, near floor level, through a slot in the concrete wall and is heated as it rises through the narrow space between the glazing and the wall. It re-enters the space through slots at ceiling height. Circulation through the room is by gravity convection. In summer, the narrow space is vented at the eave. When gravity convection does not suffice, four small fans are employed.

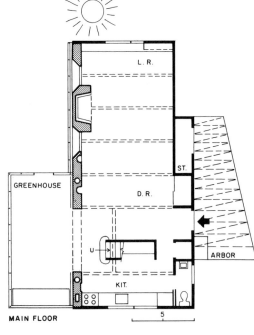

MAIN FLOOR

sultant heat loss, by conventional analysis is about 75,000 Btu per hour—32,000 of which are lost to the small greenhouse on the south face of the building. After double glazing this greenhouse, and fitting it with rolling shades, the loss should be considerably less next winter. Other adjustments and fine tuning will follow to balance temperature differentials between upstairs and down. With refreshing candor, Kelbaugh says that if he were beginning again, he would enlarge the eave vents and/or install operable windows in the south wall to increase cross ventilation.

As the photos amply indicate, the Kelbaugh house is much more than just a struggle for energy efficiency. Though it is frankly experimental, it is nonetheless a tightly disciplined piece of design with the kind of apparent simplicity that only comes with close study and careful refinement. Questions raised by its presence among the more indulgent residential forms of the past must be measured against the lessons it can yield to those interested in a less energy-extravagant future.

KELBAUGH HOUSE, Princeton, New Jersey. Architect: *Douglas Kelbaugh*. Contractor: *Nathan Bard*.

Robert Perron photos

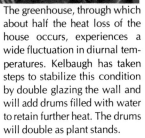

The greenhouse, through which about half the heat loss of the house occurs, experiences a wide fluctuation in diurnal temperatures. Kelbaugh has taken steps to stabilize this condition by double glazing the wall and will add drums filled with water to retain further heat. The drums will double as plant stands.

The simplest shape of all:
The ubiquitous box.
You can add to it,
cut shapes out of it

Nothing, of course, is simpler to build than the box. That has been known since some of man's earliest building, especially in arid climates where there is no need for the roof to shed rain and snow. And, with today's new materials, a flat roof is not a real problem anywhere. The simplicity of the form has also fascinated architects since the Modern movement began, and as a result the variations on the theme are now almost endless. A few are shown in this chapter, beginning with a house by Booth and Nagle that is almost a cube (the most space for the least surface)— except that the architects "had some fun" that makes this house far from ordinary: it is turned at a small angle from the "expected" parallel to the street, and, inside, that angle is repeated in openings through the floors to all three levels, creating an unexpected amount of visual interest and excitement.

A second simple square was given great interest by architects Crites and McConnell by the way the house was fitted to the site and by the addition of an entryway and garage, as shown on page 44.

The third house shown (page 46), by Hartman-Cox, is seemingly complex; yet, it is essentially a simple rectangle, with spaces inside set at varying levels to create rooms of different heights, and with windows and decks set in and out to create varied outlooks and outdoor spaces. The architects call it an "elaborate box."

Mayers & Schiff's addition to a Connecticut farmhouse (page 56) is a contemporary version of the old New England trick of "adding on."

Architect David Specter's design (page 58) uses "overhanging and cut-away sections of the second floor to give a sense of complexity within a simple framework"

Increasing complexity—combining several essentially simple shapes to create seemingly non-simple houses, and creating varied spaces inside by manipulation of levels and openings—is shown in the houses on pages 58 and 62.

And if "the box" is a simple shape, that is not to say that it cannot also be extremely sophisticated—as the elegant and exquisitely detailed house by Richard Meier shows so very well.

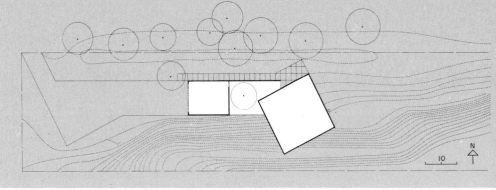

On a lot only 66 feet wide and sloping steeply to the south and west, architects Booth & Nagle designed this "cube" house for a doctor and his family in Des Moines, Iowa. The garage and entry wall parallel the contours but the main portion of the house is twisted 27½ degrees off this axis to take advantage of views to the garden and the ravine as well as to animate the simple massing. But even in the main house the contour axis is echoed in splayed partitions and non-rectilinear volumes.

The levels split at the entry: half a flight down to the kitchen, dining and living spaces; half a flight up to the master bedroom. Children's rooms and lounge occupy the uppermost level. Though a kind of zon-

ing is clearly present, all these spaces interlock vertically as the plan opposite shows.

The simple forms of the exterior are restated inside but with functional complications that add interest and visual enrichment. Color is used selectively but emphatically so that its design impact is not squandered. Nothing, in fact, is wasted. The furnishings are also selected carefully to achieve a sense of easy upkeep and pleasant understatement. The detailing is elegant but direct—a virtue consistent with the basic design goals.

The major materials are stucco for exterior finish, oak for flooring and trim, steel for sash and sliding door assemblies. The roof is built-up. Vertical glazing occurs at

the corners of the house, a design device that washes white interior walls with daylight, giving the interior spaces an especially appealing quality of light.

Thanks to simple volumetric construction and detailing and the sparing use of expensive finishes, this exceptionally handsome house was constructed for a quite moderate amount—the difficulty of the site notwithstanding.

PRIVATE RESIDENCE, Des Moines, Iowa. Architects: *Booth & Nagle—Marvin Ullman, job captain.* Engineers: *Weisenger-Holland* (structural), *Wallace & Midgal, Inc.* (mechanical). Contractor: *Byran Crow.*

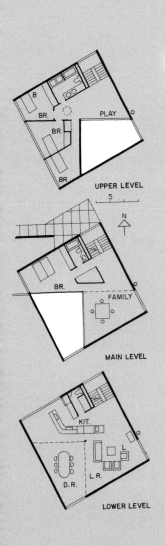

UPPER LEVEL

5

N

MAIN LEVEL

LOWER LEVEL

The architects have softened the effect of a determinedly angular scheme by introducing a gentle curve in the flow of cabinets around the partition that separates the kitchen and dining space (photos below). The contrast is unexpected but appropriate and pleasant.

Bill Hedrich, Hedrich-Blessing photos

2

On a rolling wooded site in Burlington, Iowa, architects Crites & McConnell designed this unusually handsome house for an active family of four. The site's natural contours fall abruptly to the north and east so the architects anchored the garage and entry at the uppermost level, then let the main portion of the house reach out over the slope. Living room, dining room and kitchen occupy the upper level and open across a narrow deck toward the northeast and distant views of a small river. A sub-system of dropped beams—some in the plane of the interior partitions—carries the fascia line of the garage through the taller portions of the upper level. Bedrooms are located on the level below, share the same orientation,

yet remain 11 feet above grade due to the sharp slope of the lot.

Over the concrete foundations, the house is wood frame and clad in cedar siding. Interior partitions are finished in dry wall, ceilings are cedar deck upstairs and gypsum board in the bedrooms below. Floors are carpeted and occasionally the carpet is turned up to provide finish surface for partitions. Heating and air-conditioning are gas-fired forced air.

Some of the editors felt reservations about the detailing of the Walworth house—particularly in the way that girders sheathed in plywood seemed, in the exterior photographs, to suggest steel spandrels. What they all agreed, however, is that the

Walworth house achieves a remarkable degree of design interest without straining and with a commendable economy of means. The planning is intelligent, the sitework restrained but effective, the massing simple but interesting. The spaces inside are ordered in strict rectilinear volumes but have more than ample variety of spatial feeling and flow in and out with uncontrived ease. In a word, the Walworth house does everything a good house should, and does it gently and modestly but with a clear sense of design conviction.

LEN WALWORTH RESIDENCE, Burlington, Iowa. Architects: *Crites & McConnell*. Contractor: *Schofield & Son Construction Company*.

MAIN LEVEL

N

UT.

D.R.

K.

STOR.

L.R.

LOWER LEVEL   5

BR.

BR.

BR.

Joel Strasser photos

This house in Potomac, Maryland, was designed as an "elaborate box," says Warren Cox of Hartman-Cox Architects. While this might seem an oversimplified statement, it is in fact a most accurate description—for a high, rectilinear form that steps down its site proved to be the best response to the site which offered abundant light and a steep slope. These site conditions combined with the client's specific space requirements required an intricately designed spatial arrangement. No attempt was made to break up the form's horizontality, and indeed it is emphasized on the south elevation (above) by a complex interplay of solid and open planes. The enclosed and private upper portion of the house, bridging the more transparent lower levels, and an unchanging roof line, are the dominating linear elements.

The southern elevation is a complex study of contrasting effects of materials and light and shadow, particularly demonstrated and experienced at night. A large circular window in the east elevation (below) is the only non-square form in the house and does add variety, but is perhaps more importantly an unexpected playful element. As an extension of this whimsey, an exposed steel beam crosses through the window.

The 4,000-square-foot house for a family of four is positioned in a natural clearing on a wooded three-acre site in a suburb of Washington, D.C. Terracing the house on the steeply sloping site was a logical solution not only to make best use of the topography, but to meet the client's request that the main living spaces be open and separated only by levels or partial screens and oriented to the south and east with extensive use of glass. Well proportioned overhangs shield the glass walls in the summer, and trees near the house filter the sunlight in the spring and fall but permit winter sunlight to

stream into the house. An outstretched wall of storage cabinets screens the porte-cochere and directs views to the lower portion of the site.

The heart of the design solution is the deliberate separation of spatial functions between the lower, terraced levels housing the "public" spaces—the living, sitting, and dining rooms, and the kitchen; and the second-story "private" areas—mainly bedrooms. The carefully designed juxtaposition of materials, color and forms creates a noticeable separation between these zones—particularly when viewed from the exterior. The main living spaces are open and flow freely into each other—both horizontally and vertically—as the floor levels and therefore the volumes of space change.

The private areas are enclosed in a rigid rectangle, seemingly suspended overhead, with little transparency and a gray-colored cedar exterior.

The tallest interior space is the living room, which has ground-level windows only on the east but receives a light through clerestory windows on two sides, and the unexpected round window.

Because of the extensive glass in the wall the structure is supported on that side by steel columns and beams left exposed to maintain the integrity of the openness; the rest of the house is conventional wood-frame construction.

Private residence, Potomac, Maryland. Architect: Hartman-Cox Architects—David Jones, project assistant. Engineers: James M. Cutts & Associates (structural), Ayers-Williams-Dodd (mechanical). Interior designs: Ann Hartman. Contractor: Leo T. Thibodeau.

FOURTH LEVEL

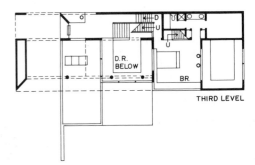

THIRD LEVEL

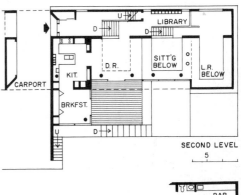

SECOND LEVEL

5

FIRST LEVEL

The sitting room (left) and the other main living space occupy most of the terraced levels, each separated by only a few steps. The living room can be seen just beyond the sitting room. The spaces are open and flow together, connected by a stairway spine open from the entrance located near the porte-cochere. The dining room (below), one level above the sitting room, has a view through the high-volumed spaces of both the sitting and living rooms. A window bordering the master bedroom looks out to the dining area.

Ezra Stoller Associates © Esto

4 Adults and children each have a two-story suite in this house in Westport, Connecticut, designed for an artist and his family by Weiner and Gran in association with Davis, Brody and Associates. The two elements intersect at the entrance and share kitchen and dining room. For the children, the corridor leads past bedrooms to a stair down to the recreation room and a terrace on grade. For the parents, an entry-gallery for the display of paintings leads to a two-story living room that looks into the woods. Also from the gallery, a stair climbs to the spacious study–master-bedroom suite. A projecting wing wall (right) screens the stair from view in the living room. Care was taken with many such details to present a neutral background for the paintings which are the most important elements of the room. The original owner also worked in stained glass and mirrored surfaces. Two examples of such work appear in the study (right): the windows above the entry and the mirrored column next to the desk. Specially-designed lighting highlights the constantly changing collection of art works.

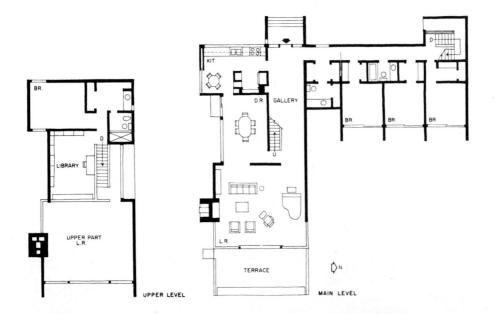

UPPER LEVEL

MAIN LEVEL

Associated architects: Davis, Brody and Associates and Weiner Gran Associates. *Location:* Westport, Connecticut, *Engineers:* Andrew Elliot (structural); Wald and Zigas (mechanical). *Landscape architect:* A. E. Bye. *Contractor:* Michael Sochaki.

5

The owners already had a small and no-longer-adequate house on this property when they commissioned Richard Meier to help them examine their building options. After study, the decision was taken to treat the new structure as freestanding and self-sufficient, but to retain the existing structure as a pool house and guest annex.

As privacy requirements on this thickly-treed site were scant, Meier strove to make the new house as open as possible. The entry is on the uphill side across a narrow, playfully detailed bridge. From this arrival point, overlooking the main living spaces, the entire interior volume is revealed—as is the relationship between the house and its sloping site. The Meier design idiom—the white planar surfaces, the exquisite pipe rail sculptures, the absolutely minimal detail—are all here in their now familiar forms but with at least one important variation. In this house, the architect has introduced a series of gentle baroque curves that play against the otherwise severe rectilinear geometry with much more than mere esoteric effect. The deck, extending the master bedroom to the outside, is one such curve. The imprint on the fireplace breast is another. The main stair, leading from the entry landing to the living room is a third. The stair's gentle curve carries the visitor around a protruding pipe column, heightening its presence, and putting visual pressure on the living room space. The flow of space through the rest of the house is almost uninterrupted except that the upstairs study is kept rather private.

This house makes a family with the Smith, Weinstein and Douglas houses. To Meier, they represent a completed body of work, a theme with variations extended and examined rather fully.

Any new houses, says Meier, will explore some new themes.

Architect: Richard Meier & Associates
  136 East 57th Street
  New York City
Engineers:
  Severud Perrone Sturm Bandel (structural)
  Thomas Polise (mechanical)
Contractor: Walmara Construction
Photographer: Ezra Stoller © ESTO

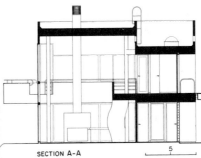

SECTION A-A

The structure in this house is a combination of steel tube columns and conventional wood frame. The floors are finished in oak strip; walls and ceilings are finished gypsum board. Exterior finishes are glass and vertical cedar siding.

6

Here is an 80-year-old, rural house in Connecticut that has undergone minor cosmetic surgery several times in the past. None of these revisions, however, provided what was needed most: an adequate living room keyed to lawn spaces and to distant views. The existing living room was little more than an access way to the stairs and was virtually unfurnishable.

Mayers & Schiff strove to retain as much of the original character of the house as possible but to express the new addition for what it was. No attempt has been made to visually incorporate the new into the old or to erase the seam. The new living room is a double-height volume placed at 45 degrees to existing axes. It encloses at its upper level the existing eaves together with windows. Only the lower portion of the existing wall was removed and replaced with a structural column. In this manner, the old projects quite literally into the new, serving as a constant, vestigial reminder of what was, and making the new work an addition in the purest sense. To further emphasize the relationship between old and new, the existing horizontal siding was retained and contrasted to new finishes which are laid up diagonally.

The 45-degree offset of the addition opens direct views to the distant hills of the southeast and to large trees and lawn to the southwest—views that previously had been obliques.

There was, of course, a good deal of fun in the design to begin with. Mayers & Schiff retained much of it and added some of their own; but they were careful, in doing so, to solve real problems of comfort and function as well.

RESIDENTIAL ADDITION, Connecticut. Architects: *Mayers & Schiff.* Owners: *Martin and Lois Nadel.* Contractor: *Clifford Taber.*

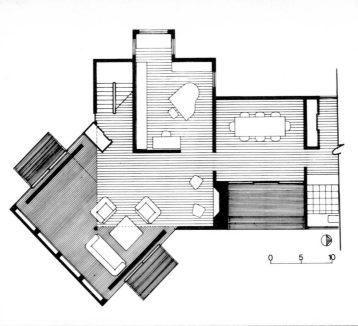

Bill Maris photos

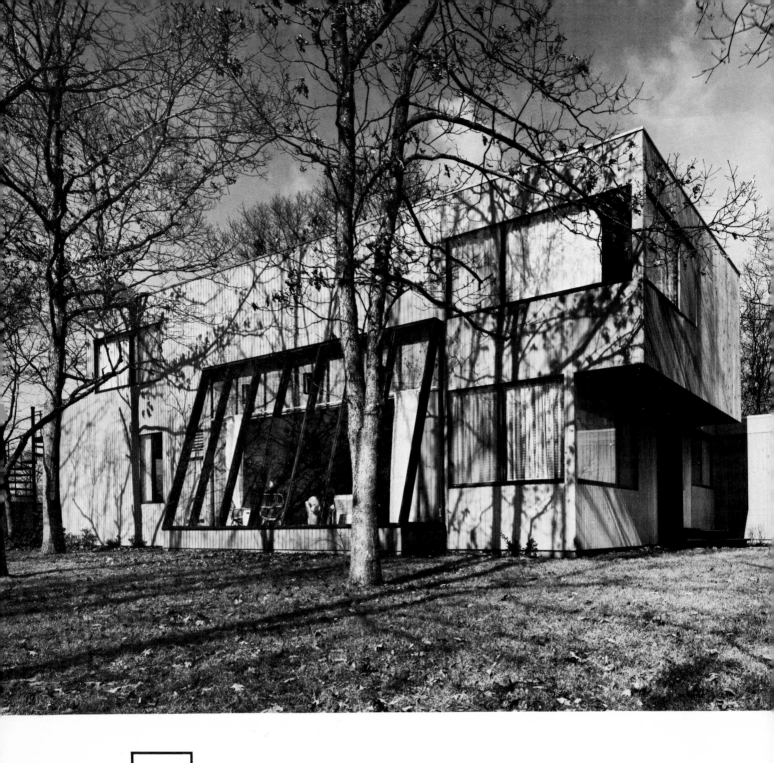

7 In his design for this house, architect David Specter has managed a series of contrasts —light open areas against closed private areas, serenity but surprise, restraint in form and color and detailing set off against a number of visual spectaculars.

The box forms of the house blend quietly with the wooded site, but overhanging and cut-away sections of the second floor give a sense of complexity within a simple framework. The house is entered on an essentially blank side (see plan) and was designed, in Specter's words "as a linear experience, with a succession of spaces opening both vertically and horizontally off a main 'spine'."

Just past the low-ceilinged entry area—closed on one side by a blank wall and on the other by a two-sided fireplace—the space opens broadly on both sides (page 59) to the dining room on the right and the living room to the left. The eye is drawn upwards by the stair to the high ceiling of the living room and central well. This explosion of scale is redoubled by the sloping glass wall of the living room and by the sloping glass skylight at the stairwell. The effect, as the interior photos show in part, is a rare and changing quality of light in this dramatic central portion of the house.

Materials were selected for low maintenance. The cedar plywood exterior and factory-finished aluminum window frames require no painting. The warm pine ceilings throughout the house, like the monochromatic wall colors, help set off the clients' art collection.

Architect: DAVID KENNETH SPECTER
2061 Broadway, New York City
Location: East Hampton, New York
Engineers: R. Howard Sanford (structural); Walter Rabadan and Martin Morse (mechanical); Joseph Petraglia (electrical)
Landscape architect: R. T. Schnadelbach
Interior designer: Dolores Engle
Contractor: Peter Wazlo

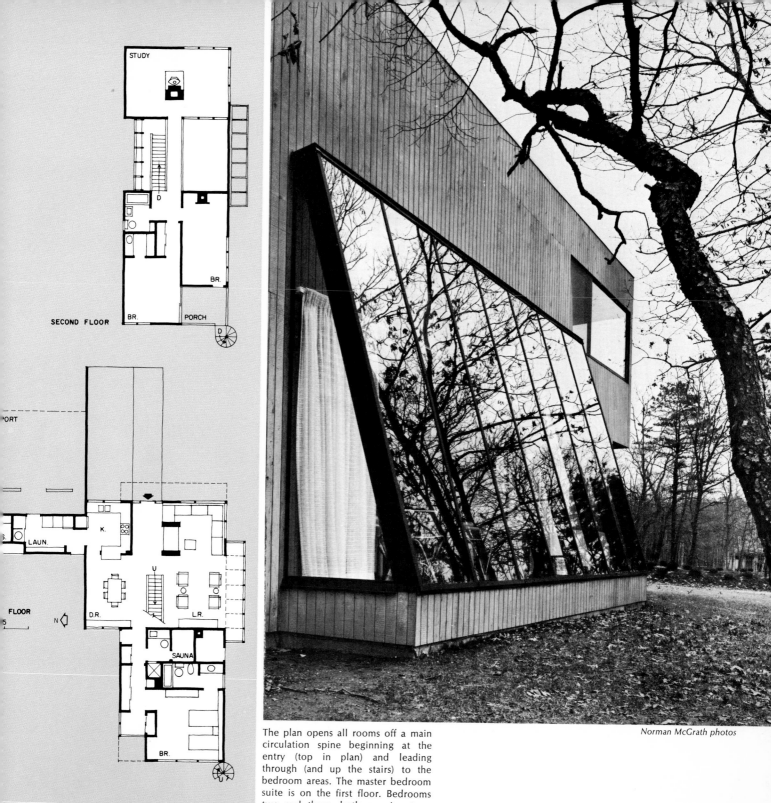

STUDY

BR.

SECOND FLOOR

BR.   PORCH

PORT

LAUN.   K.

FLOOR   N

D.R.   L.R.

SAUNA

BR.

The plan opens all rooms off a main circulation spine beginning at the entry (top in plan) and leading through (and up the stairs) to the bedroom areas. The master bedroom suite is on the first floor. Bedrooms two and three, both opening to a porch, are above.

Norman McGrath photos

On the interior, architect Specter's design offers constant changes of scale, horizontally and vertically. The living room, left, has a quiet corner tucked under the study (balcony at top). The bridge shown in the photos on this page serves the study, which the client wished "psychologically remote" from the rest of the house. The tongue-and-groove pine ceilings throughout the house cast a warm light on the rooms and reinforce the flow of space.

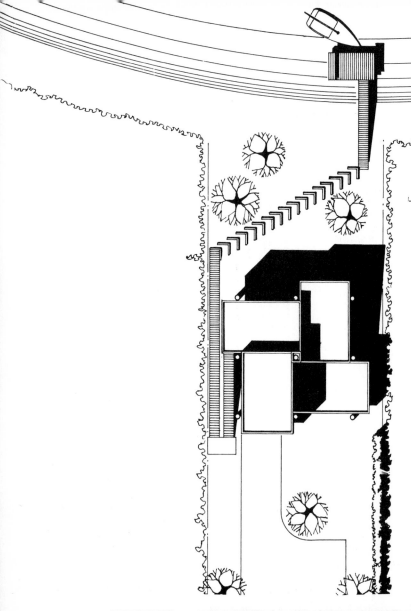

N

10

8

Because of its exposed structure and woodwork, this house seems to have been made by a loving craftsman. Details and materials are articulated in a way that conveys something very well-made.

Like a pier over low water the house extends between pilings out over a lakeside slope. It is raised off the ground as part of "a preservationist approach" says architect William Morgan. This minimized earthwork and thus minimized disturbance or destruction of trees, leaves a tree canopy which, with the house sited well up on the slope, provides privacy for the rooms open to the lake. The house presents a blank aspect to the road (photo below) and sides, also for privacy.

As the client-contractor—a forestry professor—and his wife wanted maximum use of natural wood, the structure is almost en-

G. Wade Swicord photo

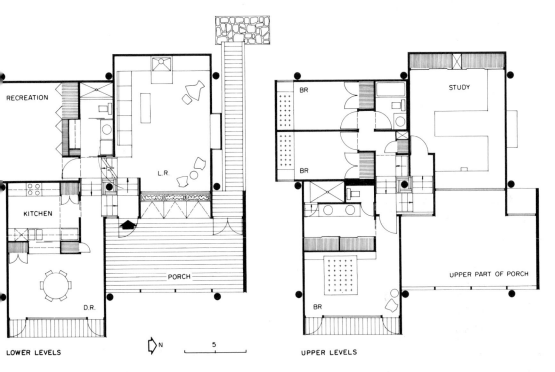

RECREATION

L.R.

KITCHEN

PORCH

D.R.

BR

BR

STUDY

UPPER PART OF PORCH

BR

N

5

LOWER LEVELS

UPPER LEVELS

irely of wood. Nine southern yel-low pine pilings are embedded to a depth of 10 feet in cylinders of poured-in-place concrete. The car-port-entry slab (under living room) is anchored to the pilings which are exposed inside and out. As they taper irregularly, they are fastened with special adjustable bolts (permitting a 2-inch variation in piling diameter) to laminated beams supporting exposed floor

and ceiling joists, all of southern yellow pine. The darkness of the treated pilings and their natural shape contrast with the crisp, machine-cut lines and light tones of rough-sawn cedar plywood sid-ing applied like clapboards and chosen for its dimensional stability.

The house consists of eight levels within four rectangular vol-umes spiraling in a pinwheel con-figuration around the central piling.

Entry is from the carport at the base of the stair or by ramp up to the two-story porch. From the porch one may go up to the living room, children's rooms, master bedroom and studio; or down to kitchen and dining room and guest-recreation room.

The plan is very compact and neatly accommodates all program requirements including "separate dining room; screened porch over-

looking lake; guest suite independ-ent of main house; studio for writ-ing and print framing; covered parking accessible to kitchen; liv-ing room suitable for displaying rare maps, prints and paintings." The last item, along with a need for privacy, resulted in a set-back wall with windows at either end. There is no hall except on the two-bedroom level as all other rooms are entered directly from

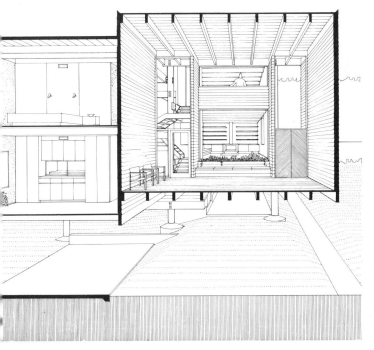

the stairwell. Every major space has a view of the lake.

Luan mahogany was used in the master bedroom paneling, interior doors and cabinet work. Southern yellow pine is also used in the door frames and the laminated, edge-grain ceilings and floors which are made of 12-inch-wide tongue-and-groove sections that are cut to the specified length—a type of flooring used in bowling alleys and vans.

As in previous houses by the same architect, simple, rectilinear volumes, expressed inside and out, combine to provide a strong sense of spatial liveliness.

PRIVATE RESIDENCE, Central Florida. Architect: *William Morgan;* structural engineer: *Haley W. Keister;* interiors: *Edward Heist, Jr.*

Larger houses are often collections of boxes–and the trick is to tie them together skillfully

This concept is clearly seen in the house overleaf by architects Smith and Yauch. A collection of simple shapes are combined to create a house that is beautifully zoned for privacy and enjoyment of the site and the view. Even the outdoor spaces—a private terrace off the master bedroom and a larger outdoor space off the living room—have their dimensions outlined by suggestions of structure.

In the Gray house (page 72), this "collection of boxes" idea is best understood in the photographs. Inside, as the architect explains, "the house is a progression of spaces that move from large gathering areas to smaller, more private ones, laced together with hallways. As the photos show, the various 'boxes' or 'the progression of spaces' are expressed by shed roofs set at different angles, not just to scoop in light, but to announce that 'this is a different space' . . ."

In the very large house by architect Paul Thoryk (page 76), the living spaces are organized into zones off a long central hallway. While this is a subtle and complex "collection of boxes," it can be read from the plan and the photos. As in the Gray house, it uses sloping roofs to express that "this is a different space."

You can trace this kind of development of basically simple square and rectangular "boxes" in all of the relatively complex houses shown through the rest of this chapter—sometimes in an urban house, like Thomas Simmon's addition to his own house (page 80); sometimes developed into an essentially farmhouse form, like the Smotrich and Platt house (page 84); sometimes in a carefree beach house, like the DeVido house (page 88); sometimes into a much more formal and almost neoclassical residence, like the strong masonry house by architects Twitchell and Miao (page 98); sometimes used to make a relatively small house seem large, as in Alfred DeVido's design (page 102); and sometimes—as in Paul Rudolph's design (page 90) and Donald Mallow's design (page 92)—to give enormous, sprawling, and especially dramatic houses a sense of human scale and a comprehensible progression that truly make them timeless modern houses.

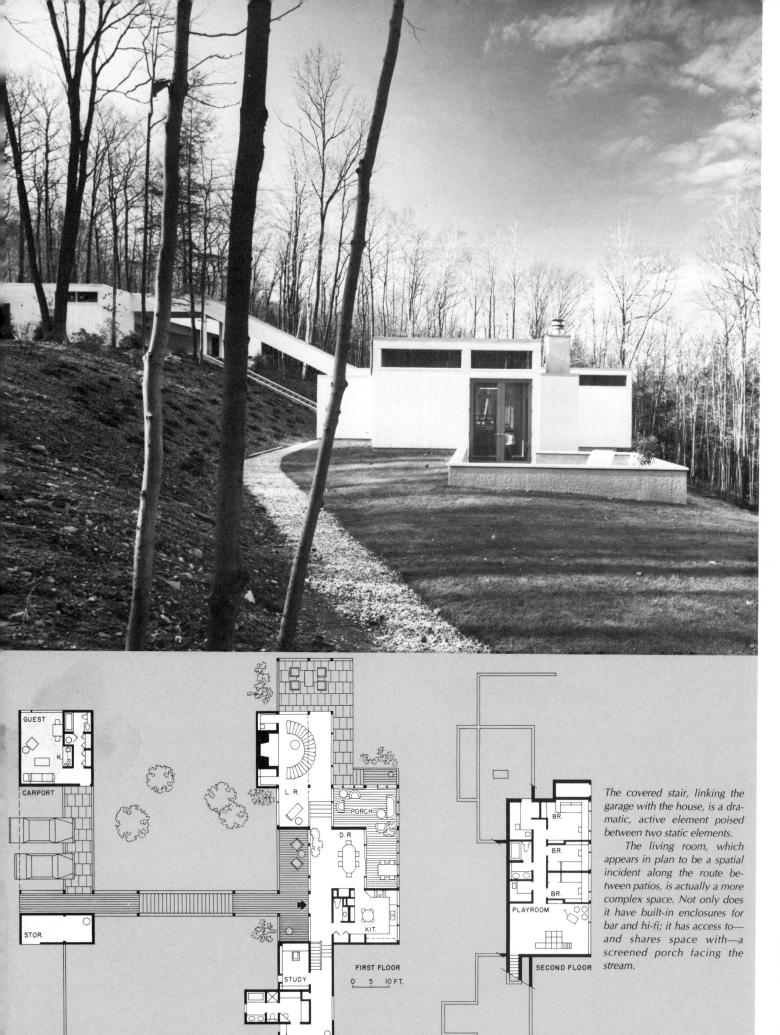

FIRST FLOOR

0 5 10 FT.

SECOND FLOOR

The covered stair, linking the
garage with the house, is a dramatic, active element poised
between two static elements.

The living room, which
appears in plan to be a spatial
incident along the route between patios, is actually a more
complex space. Not only does
it have built-in enclosures for
bar and hi-fi; it has access to—
and shares space with—a
screened porch facing the
stream.

1

Stepping down the north slope of a Massachusetts hillside—a hillside dominated by groves of birch and a stream at its base—this carefully tailored vacation house was designed for a young couple with two pre-school-age children. To use the slope effectively required a substantial system of retaining walls, which extend beyond the house east and west to embrace small outdoor patios. These extensions, together with the structures on the upper level, anchor the design securely in three directions and, from every vantage point, make the house seem larger than it actually is.

The long, linear plan of the house implies a horizontal zoning, which the architects achieved simply by introducing sliding doors at points along the gallery that make it possible to close off one or more areas of the house when not in use. Vertical zoning separates the parents' level from the children's level below. A guest room, with private kitchenette, is located next to the carport on the upper level offering guests an unusual—and sometimes welcome—degree of seclusion.

The framing is a modified post-and-beam system with 3-inch fir roof decking spanning the nine feet between beams. The exterior walls are cedar boards stained to a gray-white, interior partitions are ⅝-inch plasterboard. Operable windows are casement or awning and all openings are double-glazed. Generous openings on the south side of the house assure sunlight in the interiors at all times of day and at all seasons.

The areas around the house are seeded with grass, a decision that leaves little ambiguity between what is natural and what is designed. As the site is thickly wooded and had little in the way of view, the owners are opening a vista down to the stream that will be dammed to form a small pond. The remainder of the property will remain untouched.

Architects:
  Melvin Smith/Noel Yauch
  157 State Street
  Brooklyn, New York
Private residence
Location: Northern Massachusetts
Engineers:
  Antony Vairamides (structural)
  Lehr Associates (mechanical)
  George Maynard (site)
Landscape architect: Matthew Tomich
Contractor: Gordon Houldesworth
Photographer: David Hirsch

PRIVATE
RESIDENCE BY
MELVIN SMITH/NOEL YAUCH

Though the house is designed for heavy use in the summertime, only the master bedroom suite is air-conditioned. Breezes (with adequate cross-ventilation) do the rest.

The long gallery, photo opposite page, provides large areas for wall display. Because it is open at both ends and includes a substantial change of level, the gallery is spatially lively along its full length.

2

A house of immaculate, precise lines, this is an elegant expression that befits both entertaining and the down-to-earth functional necessity for a family of six. To fill the spatial needs for both privacy and interaction of family members, architect Paul Gray (of Warner and Gray architects) designed his own house as a "progression of spaces that move from large gathering areas to smaller more private ones, laced together with hallways."

To enhance privacy, the spaces are separated according to their function, reaching out in three directions from the entrance (upper right). The bedroom wing (right) which consumes the bulk of the 4,200 square feet, is to the north and is part of the family-centered areas, while the formal living room is completely set off to the south. This portion has the dominant geometric form of the house—the shed roof—angled to accommodate solar energy collector panels.

Because the house is located on a three-acre hillside site near the coast, the house is oriented to frame views in all directions—to the north, the mountains; to the south, the ocean; and surrounding the house, eucalyptus trees.

An integral part of the crispness of the design is the subtle separation of horizontal and vertical planes. Viewed from the exterior, the house appears to "float," being slightly raised on a concrete slab foundation and is recessed from the perimeter walls: this recess is visually emphasized by use of dark-colored stones around the base. This idea of articulation is expressed in the interiors through reveals at the junction of walls with floor and ceilings, painted a dark color, again for emphasis.

Architect: Paul Gray
  of Warner-Gray
  1225 Coast Village Road
  Santa Barbara, California
Owners: Mr. & Mrs. Paul Gray
Engineers:
  Theodore Anvick (structural/foundation)
  Leo Kummer (mechanical)
Landscape architects:
  Richard Harrington, Dick Gilbert, Paul Gray
Interior design:
  Paul Gray, Jack Warner, Gwen Warner
Contractor:
  A. O. Pieper (general)
Photographer: Charles White

One strong visual element in the design is a split fireplace (all photos left) which frames views of trees from the living room and maintains the proper scale for that section of the house, both inside and out. Of necessity, long hallways connect the multitude of rooms, but there is always a vista opened at the end, such as seen along the kitchen corridors (top and bottom). Clerestory windows abound, including in the family room (right).

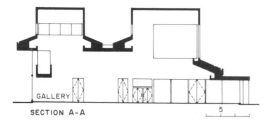
GALLERY

SECTION A-A 5

In an unusually large house (10,000 square feet including a detached guest house) architect Paul Thoryk successfully balanced the conflicting natures of a formal design concept with the informal lifestyle of Southern California. As a result of the client's program, a multi-faceted form developed, first experienced at the entrance (above). The high-volumed spaces (left) particularly signal the essential qualities of the design—an articulated form providing a variety of light-filled spaces.

A multi-faceted form for this house evolved as a visual expression of the client's desire for privacy, a directive that affects all aspects of the design. The house was positioned on its corner lot to open onto an inner courtyard (above) away from the street, from which only the garage and upper portions of the house are visible behind landscaping and a high wall. Privacy is enhanced by locating the guest rooms, maid's quarters, library and garage in a detached unit (not shown).

The interior spaces are organized into living "zones" branching off a central hallway.

These zones are reflected and emphasized on the exterior through a combination of distinctive recesses, overhangs and geometric variations—what Thoryk refers to as having an "outdoor pavilion character." A particularly articulated form, it is marked by high-volumed sections with clerestory windows, and curvilinear walls which jut out at four points around the house, offsetting the over-all rectilinear shapes while enclosing a variety of interior functions. (One encloses the children's "fun" room, another the mechanical systems, one contains a garden and one directs views from

the dining room into the formal garden, separating this area from an outdoor pool adjacent to the playroom.) For sun control on the south, large overhangs, supported by exposed concrete columns, were designed to shade the extensive glass walls.

Privacy between zones is created by the arrangement and separation of functions off the central corridor, the most obvious of which is the division between the master bedroom and the children's playroom and second-story bedrooms. It is, rather, the varied proportions and use of glass and light which announce the

The angular design elements express a deliberate effort to separate interior spatial functions, but it is design subtleties of volume, light and materials that soften the form. The living room (right) is indicative of these characteristics with its sloping ceiling, changes of floor level, and borrowing of light from the corridor. Resawn cedar was used on both the exterior and interior walls.

different zones. Each of these devices also direct views outward, to either the formal courtyard, pool, small patios or to a tennis court beyond the kitchen. These are all filled with major examples of sculpture from the owner's private collection.

PRIVATE RESIDENCE, Southern California. Architects: *Paul Thoryk and Associates—Paul Thoryk, principal-in-charge*. Engineers: *Robert Fefferman* (structural), *Stone Brothers* (foundation/soils). Landscape architect: *The Peridian Group*. Interior design/lighting/graphics consultant: *K.S. Wilshire, Inc.* General contractor: *Roland Sylvestre*.

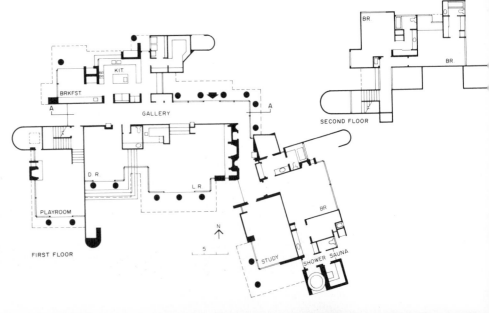

The spine of the house is a gallery (above), 40 feet long, but broken into two volumes of space each 36 feet high (see section). It is flooded with natural light through large, clerestory windows, and augmented with recessed ceiling lights for display of part of the owner's private art collection. An indoor/outdoor relationship, typical of Southern California living has been created throughout the house with glass walls and sliding-glass doors opening onto patios. For example there is a long view through the gallery to a garden (above) and to the large courtyard through the living room (right).

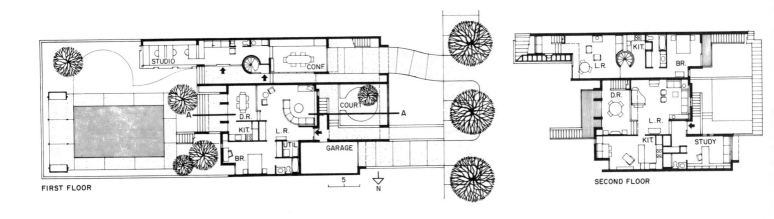

FIRST FLOOR

STUDIO

CONF

A · A

D.R.

KIT. · L.R. · COURT

UTIL

BR. · GARAGE

5 · N

SECOND FLOOR

L.R. · KIT. · BR.

D.R.

L.R.

KIT. · STUDY

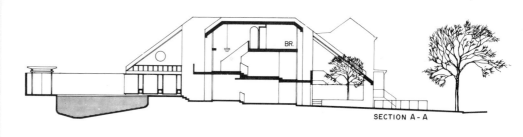

SECTION A-A

4

A decade ago, architect Thomas B. Simmons purchased a vacant lot in southeast Washington, D.C., and built a townhouse for his family that included in its design a single, lower-floor rental unit. He then went to work in a local firm. When he decided recently to open his own practice, Simmons bought an adjacent lot and made a substantial addition to his earlier house. The new addition includes his office on the ground floor, a new master bedroom above and a second rental unit, this time a small duplex, also over the office.

The architect describes the situation as ''a kind of affluent commune with none of the messy, shared privacies so mistakenly undertaken by real communes—each unit has complete separation, just the amenities are shared.'' These amenities are not inconsiderable. They include a handsome swimming pool and garden for flowers and vegetables, all arranged in the consolidated backyard space (photo right).

The new office space (photo overleaf) faces the pool and is generously north lighted through glass walls that keep the narrow linear volume from feeling constricted. Operable panels admit pleasant summer breezes.

For his new wing, Simmons has freely introduced new forms and details—especially new kinds of openings—but collected them under the same metal roof and integrated them easily into a single, united composition. A lot happens in these volumes but the spaces do not seem tortured and the functions (house, rental apartments, office) are carefully organized to complement each other in a variety of ways.

SIMMONS RESIDENCE AND OFFICE, Washington, D.C. Architect: *Thomas B. Simmons*. Structural engineer for addition: *Carl Hansen*. Landscape architect: *Ferco Goldinger*. Contractor for addition: architect/owner.

The dining space (photo left) and the office (photo across page) both focus on the pool and garden at the rear of the property. The new master bedroom (photo below) overlooks the entry court. The narrow conference area (photo right) is an extension of the drafting area that opens through a wheel window to the same entry court.

5 In response to a generous site—25 hilly acres partly wooded and partly open— and the needs of a large family, architects Charles Platt and David Smotrich have created a rambling and beautifully planned house. The client was familiar with, and began by wanting a traditional frame house with rooms of conventional box-like form. The architects' solution is a house that is quietly modern but, with its shingles, clapboards, shed roofs, extended plan and reminiscent wood detailing, has the spirit of a New England farmhouse.

The total compound was designed to accommodate a family with six children, dogs, horses, two cars, a truck and tractor. It is care-fully zoned so that the service entrance is convenient to the kitchen and utility area and the children's end is separate and may be closed off for intermittent use as the family grows older.

The landscaping is in zones related to interior functions and demarcated by walls extending beyond the building lines in a pinwheel configuration. There's an informal play area off the children's rooms; the main living areas are all oriented toward the best view; and the barn is close to the fields. One of the nicest features of the house is that all but two of the bedrooms have direct access to the outdoors.

Simple and traditional materials were used in this very large house. The exterior is cedar clapboards and shingles. The interior is gypsum wall board with some cedar ceilings and oak floors.

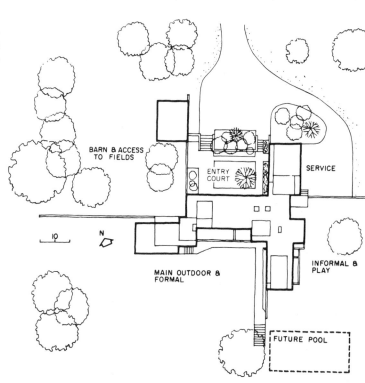

Architects: DAVID I. SMOTRICH and CHARLES A. PLATT of Smotrich & Platt
305 East 45th Street, New York, New York
Owner: Mr. & Mrs. Franklin E. Parker
Location: Mendham, New Jersey
Structural engineer: Robert Silman
Mechanical engineer: Harry H. Bond
Contractor: Maw & McKinnell

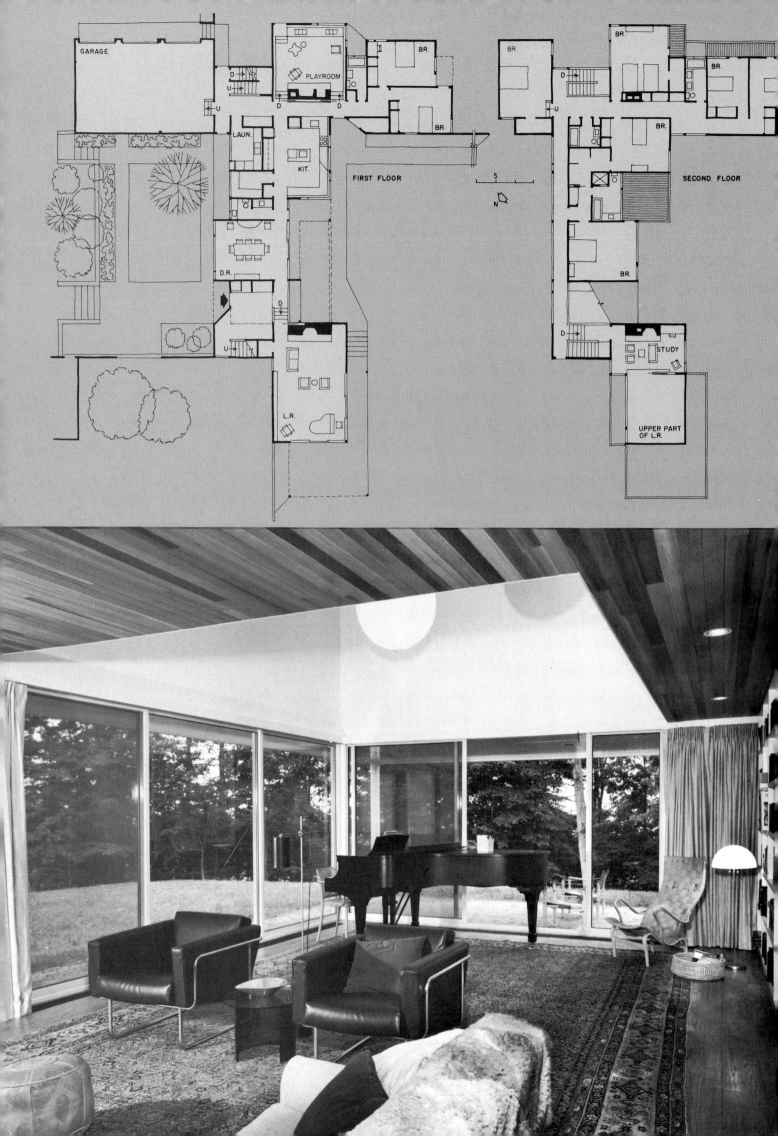

GARAGE

LAUN.

KIT.

PLAYROOM

BR.

BR.

BR.

D.R.

L.R.

FIRST FLOOR

5

N

BR.

BR.

BR.

BR.

BR.

SECOND FLOOR

STUDY

UPPER PART
OF L.R.

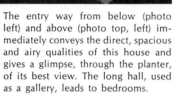

The entry way from below (photo left) and above (photo top, left) immediately conveys the direct, spacious and airy qualities of this house and gives a glimpse, through the planter, of its best view. The long hall, used as a gallery, leads to bedrooms.

The playroom (photo above) is sunk three steps below the main level of the house. It is open on the outside to the play area and at either end of the fireplace (see plan) to the kitchen. The painting near the door is by architect Charles Platt.

The Parker house living room (photos left and right) has both intimate, low, cedar-ceilinged areas and an expansive two-story space with clerestory windows. The study overlooking it may be closed off with sliding doors. The room was designed to fit the large oriental rug. The mantel, taken from the owner's former house, gives a traditional touch.

Norman McGrath photos

Ezra Stoller © ESTO phot

 6

The owners of this house required the usual living quarters plus an apartment for visiting married children, a study and a studio. In addition, they specifically requested a house in which masonry was to be the dominant structural material. Their site fronted Peconic Bay to the west and afforded the owners unobstructed views of water and distant shoreline.

De Vido strung the plan out perpendicular to the western view and recessed the glazing line to shield windows from sun and glare. Living room, dining and kitchen areas and guest apartment occupy the first floor while the upper floor is reserved for the master bedroom, study and studio. The floors are linked by a stair as well as a long ramp that continues all the way to the roof.

The primary problem, says De Vido, came in trying to combine the concrete block with wood and glass in a way that was visua[l] coherent. As finally designed, the block encloses space on three sid[es] and is set at right angles to the view on the fourth. Light wood pane[ls] serve as infill. This design decision led to the cubical volumes whic[h] give the house its characteristic massing.

The interplay of materials carries through to the interiors whi[ch] are simply but functionally expressed. Although internal spaces a[re] closely defined by walls and partitions there is more than sufficie[nt] flow of space, upward as well as outward, to excite the eye and stim[u]late the senses.

PRIVATE RESIDENCE, Long Island, New York. Architect: *Alfred De Vido.*
Contractor: *Walter King.*

7

This extraordinary house—perhaps the most visually arresting residence that Rudolph has completed to date—is designed for a family with two grown sons and a daughter. The house rises from a gently contoured waterfront site rich in tree cover and low growth.

The basic building element is a wood frame, cut and bolted into a seven-sided figure with rigid side walls set back from the edges of the frame. The enclosure that these elements create is double-cantilevered from heavy wood

posts built up of 2- by 12-inch members. The more heavily textured surface, used extensively both inside and out, is plywood with lath and a cementitious binder applied. Into this binder, while still wet, pebbles were set by trowel. The two materials are played against each other with virtuosity to create a planar/linear composition of unusual force. Like the Burroughs-Wellcome Headquarters, to which it bears a kinship both in forms and materials—and which was designed at about the same time—this house explores a rich variety of diagonal relationships. In, up, around and through, the space flows easily and almost without interruption.

Dramatic and sculptural in its intent? Certainly. Indulgent in its use of materials? Decidedly. Fer-

vently. But accepted on its own terms, it is a magnificent construction, intuitive in its logic and full of ideas carried to a degree of development and elaboration not normally within the reach of residential designers.

Architect: Paul Rudolph
  project architects:
  John Harding
  Donald Luckenbill
  54 West 57th Street
  New York, New York
Private residence
Location: New York State
Engineers: Paul Gugliotta (structural)
Contractor: Anderson Brothers
  Construction
Photographer: Y. Futigawa

The spaces of the house are developed across a series of partial levels and all turned outward to views of deck, pool and shoreline. Secondary spaces turn at right angles to form a separate wing. The upper levels of the house, varied and sometimes skylighted, are mostly bedrooms but full of the spatial invention and detail that give the rest of the house its rich, expressive character.

Norman C. McGrath photos

8

Many architects today feel that low-income housing is far more important than the design of single-family houses, especially on the grand scale of this one in Lakewood, New Jersey by Donald C. Mallow.

Architects who feel, however, that architecture must always balance delight with utility, will find these six pages immensely stimulating. There are those who will say that the owner, Robert Schmertz, who has built several "Leisure Village" retirement communities across the United States, has not cared to endow those projects, a variety of low-income housing, with architectural grace. But Schmertz is secure in the knowledge that he has given the people what they want, something architects themselves do not always do. What most architects will agree on, however, is that the realization of this house has demanded as much restraint and taste from the clients as from the designer. It is a building, one of Mallow's first as an independent practitioner, that does not rely upon innovation or design tricks for its impact. Rather it is impressive as an example of thorough mastery of a wide range of architectural ideas synthesized with clarity and intellectual economy. As any architect who has designed a large house knows, realization of the complex program can be infinitely more difficult than that for smaller houses. Traps such as misunderstood scale, much too complicated plan relationships, overly elaborate materials and finishes all can destroy the esthetic validity of the architect's intent. Mallow has avoided all of them. Designer of the interiors, furniture and landscaping as well as the building, he has produced a timeless modern house.

In the design of any house, as important as the solution of the program is the way in which the architectural forms relate to the site. Instead of placing the long axis parallel to the contours of the hillside, Mallow has tucked the private end of the house, above, with its many small rooms, into the grade and allowed the living room pavilion to stand free. A steel structural system, using 110 tons in all, not only permitted the cantilevered balconies and mitred glass corners of the pavilion, right, but on the entrance side, using an 8-inch car channel, permitted crisp fascias which clearly articulate the several changes in roof planes and which contrast with the Delaware Valley sandstone walls. Nowhere is the subtle scale, one of the most evasive architectural qualities, more obvious than on the terrace around which the house wraps. On one side the pavilion, seen at its crystalline best in the twilight. On the other, above, the master bedroom suite which gently steps down the natural grade, conveying its intimate quality. In front of the pavilion, a carp pool and a swimming pool, which seem to flow together, lie on axis with various parts of the house. These relationships, not obvious at first, tie the whole composition together in ordered serenity.

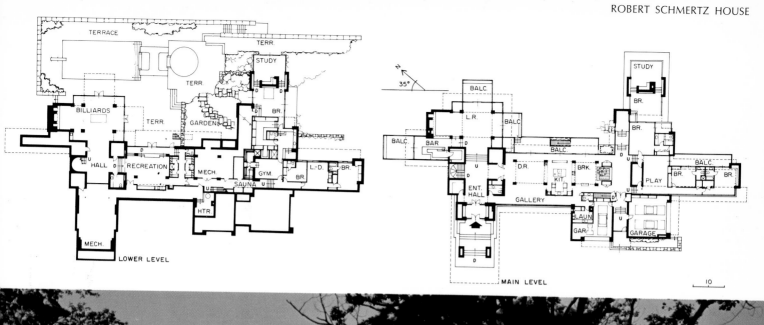

LOWER LEVEL

MAIN LEVEL

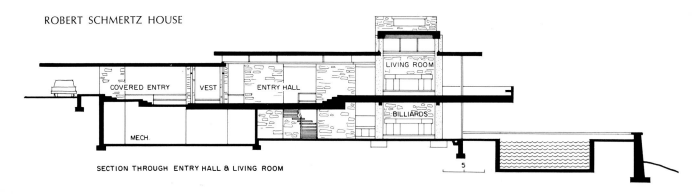

SECTION THROUGH ENTRY HALL & LIVING ROOM

Perhaps the single most interesting architectural event of the Schmertz house is the 127-foot-long axis from the porte-cochere to the balcony overlooking the swimming pool. The section above illustrates one of architect Mallow's rules for assuring a sense of order as one moves through the house: when the floor plane changes levels, the ceiling plane remains constant; the ceiling plane changes only when the floor plane is constant. From the 7-foot 6-inch ceiling at the landing to the high degree of enclosure within the vestibule, there is an increasing sense of compression. Then, when one reaches the base of the steps up to the living room, he not only sees the clerestory for the first time, but to his right can see the dining-room–kitchen axis. Yet the explosion of space that occurs when one enters the living room, above, is unexpected nonetheless. Scale, enclosure, texture of materials, careful detailing and most important, light, have been used to create a powerful example of axial composition.

The dining room, kitchen and breakfast room form the link between the public and private segments of the house. Windows around the raised roof section fill the dining and breakfast room pavilions with sunlight all day long. The dining table as well as most other pieces of furniture were designed by the architect. The kitchen, looking toward the dining room, below, is equipped to handle large dinners as well as daily needs. Facing the pools and the lake, a glazed arcade connects the dining room and the daily entrance. Sliding glass doors allow easy access to the adjacent balcony with its stair down to the multi-level terrace.

RESIDENCE FOR MR. AND MRS. ROBERT J. SCHMERTZ, Lakewood, New Jersey. Architect: *Donald C. Mallow*; engineers: *Sadler Associates (structural), Peter Bruder (mechanical)*; lighting consultant: *Donald Bliss*; interior design and landscaping: *Donald C. Mallow*; general contractor: *Robilt, Inc.*

9

Access to this 6,500-square-foot house is gained by a quarter-of-a-mile drive, bordered by a hedgerow which ends to reveal the north entrance front (opposite, above). The site comprises more than 100 acres in upper New York State, and the house's surrounds include a hayfield sloping toward views to the southwest. The building plan is organized with several setbacks on the south side, in order to give many rooms a maximum benefit of the outlook.

Architects Twitchell & Miao planned the rooms to provide a maximum of spatial variety, and zoning for privacy, while providing adequate supervision for the children. The parents' bedroom is separated from the children's by a bridge over the liv-

ing room providing a connecting link at night. As the bridge is open to a two-story-high area of the living room, it also allows vertical communication during the day (overleaf, top). The apartment over the garage will accommodate guests or a live-in couple.

''Upstate'' New York has long respected the gracious proportions of the most literal neo-classic tradition in towns named Syracuse, Ithaca and Troy. The house here would seem to be particularly appropriate to such a region in its strong—though not contrived—resemblance to the country houses of the periods that gave inspiration to nineteenth century builders. There is a solid character and a formality to

massing and openings. The ancillary b ing is linked by a wall that is an illusory tension of the main structure. A raised gia and enclosed garden offer varied looks and views are carefully contro There is a strong contrast between ''pub and garden facades.

Construction consists of conc block walls that support wood joists a floor and roof levels. Steel beams were quired to hold the block above the la windows and openings.

PRIVATE RESIDENCE, upper New York State chitects: *Twitchell & Miao—partners: Terry chell and Nancy Miao.* Engineers: *Ant Vairanudes* (structural); *Dalton & Dunne* chanical/electrical). Contractor: *Camanto, Ir*

Norman C. McGrath photos

STUDY

BR.

L.R.

D.R.

KIT.

MUD

GARAGE

FIRST FLOOR

5

N

BR.

UPPER PART
OF L.R.

PLAY

BR.

BR.

BR.

BR.

KIT.

L.R.

BR.

SECOND FLOOR

The living and dining rooms are well planned for entertaining, and they serve as a buffer between a wing for the parents and the children's area on the second floor over service areas on the first. The bridge (left and far right, top) connects the bedrooms of the two generations. Interior surfaces were planned for a minimum of maintenance and include quarry tile floors and a marble fireplace. The placement of the second floor deck affords a vantage point for views and a children's play space, while adding spatial variety to the living room.

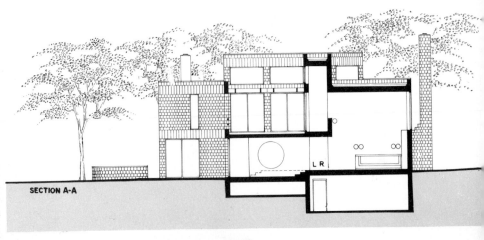

SECTION A-A

L R

Bill Maris photos

Architectural scale can be used to make big buildings seem smaller, or in this case, a small house seem quite enormous. Visitors approach the Willard Wirth house in Westchester County, near New York City, up a steep drive through tulip and maple trees. The elevation which greets them at the top (left) has little besides a standard overhead garage door to betray its true size. It was architect Alfred De Vido's intent that they be dazzled by the faceted forms, each 15 feet wide, before entering what is, in fact, a collection of cozy rooms that look out into the woods.

The architect's decision to string the units out on an east-west axis was based principally on site considerations. Two parallel fieldstone retaining walls which cross the contour lines at about 30 degrees and form the spine of his design cause the east end (below) to stand out from the grade. The garage portion (bottom opposite) on the other hand, nestles into the grade to permit adequate space for guest parking and turning. On the south-facing uphill side (below left), the land was graded up to the house slightly to keep surface drainage away. Because of the linear scheme, each room has windows to the winter sun even though their principal exposure is to the north. And in the summer, each has cross-ventilation to catch the breezes: the air along the slope moves uphill in the morning as the sun warms it—downhill at night as it cools.

Architect: ALFRED DE VIDO. *Owner:* Willard Wirth. *Location:* Westchester County, New York *Landscape architect:* A. E. Bye.

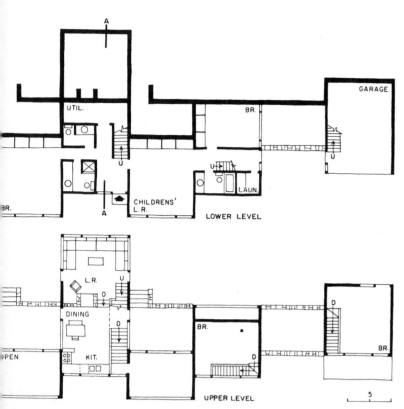

From the entry, visitors walk up one flight to the kitchen-dining room and then three more steps up to the living room. There, in a space 15 feet square, they can relax and look south across to the hill rising behind the house or climb up another flight of stairs (right) to the study above the kitchen. Like the living room, the kitchen has windows on three sides as well as access to paved courts looking down into the master bedrooms on one side and the children's living room on the other. The thorough separation of various rooms has insured a high degree of acoustical privacy for parents and children.

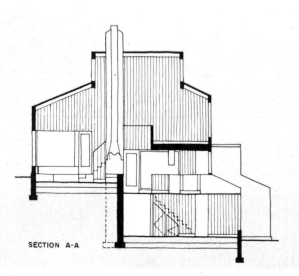

SECTION A-A

The circle: A strong geometric form that generates strong and forceful shapes for houses (though a little goes a long way)

A number of our cities now have hotels in the form of round towers—and because of the strength of the form they are hard to miss (even amidst other towers, as in Atlanta and Los Angeles). The Mall in Washington now boasts a round museum, the Hirschhorn—and if controversial, it is extremely dominant even in that great space.

Because of this strength, in houses where circular shapes are used—if for nothing more than a stair tower—the eye seems drawn there.

The first house in this chapter, by architect Richard Henderson, is essentially a simple box; yet the use of a circular form to generate a living room deck (the shape appears sparingly, though importantly, inside) dominates the design (see photos overleaf).

In the second, by architect J. Lawrence Scott, a round tower—used only to mark the entrance, creates a nook off the living room, and (upstairs) a study for the owner—catches the eye amidst a lively composition of angular massing.

In the remaining houses, the circular form is used more forcefully:

In the Koplik house (page 114), pairs of drum shapes create a strong and interesting form on an essentially featureless site. Here, the circular forms shape almost all of the rooms except, surprisingly, the living room, which is a two-story space bridging the circular forms.

In architect Stanley Tigerman's "Hot Dog House" (page 118), the circular ends of the house are conceived as making the house two sided rather than as in a box, four sided—part of Tigerman's intellectual rationale for this striking house on its wonderful site. (It is not, however, necessary to understand this rationale to appreciate that this must be a wonderful house to live in.)

Finally, for his own house, architect Peter Woerner used the circular form in elevation—to create a house which "springs from, and then returns to, the earth in a pure form—an easy and effortless arc." It is, for all of its unfamiliarity, a house that seems singularly right for its site and its views.

In words any architect would cherish, Loring Mandel wrote in *The New York Times*, December 6, 1970, of the house Richard Henderson designed for him. Speaking of his site—two acres in the middle of a 60-year old private arboretum in Huntington, Long Island—the client wrote of his hopes as the project began: "The house would not be a jewel in a setting. The valley was the jewel, and the house had to be fashioned to let us see it in bloom or in snow." Henderson had two immediate reactions to the land: first, the scheme must be linear and run along the contours to minimize its effect on the rich environment. Second, at the western end of the house, a sweeping vista into the valley was indicated rather than a directed one. The resulting plan (below) can be seen as a linear house with a semi-circular deck or, if viewed with the diagonal through the steel-framed living room as a vertical, as a glazed pavilion on a rounded terrace set in the woods with service areas, like an umbilical cord, connecting it to the outside world. Thus, with a straightforward 2300 sq ft plan and very economical use of circular geometry, Henderson has accomplished both siting goals.

Architect: RICHARD HENDERSON.
Owner: Mr. and Mrs. Loring Mandel.
Location: Huntington Bay, New York.
Engineer: Geiger-Berger (structural).
Contractor: Harry Sprukts.

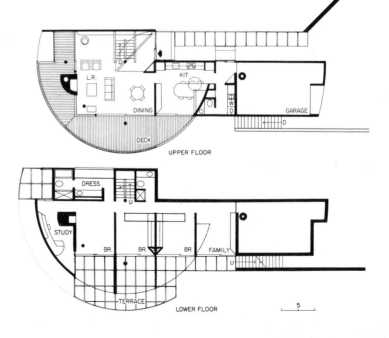

UPPER FLOOR

LOWER FLOOR

William Maris photos

Viewed from the west along the diagonal through the living room (left below), the sweep of the circular terrace is emphasized. The curving facade of the garage (below) has as its focus the same point, the column in the entry, as do the other curved walls.

The pavilion-like quality of the Mandel living-dining room is revealed when one reaches the entrance (left), a tall space which fills the room with morning sunlight. The column at the head of the stairs supports a beam which generates a forceful diagonal. It also is the pivot point for the circular terrace and other concentric circles, such as the kitchen wall (below) into which the table butts. The glazed walls of the pavilion (right), in contrast to the kitchen, are well shaded by the deep overhang. Thus, for the person looking out at the trees, sky glare is eliminated to better display ever-changing nature.

In his study (below) Loring Mandel wrote for *The New York Times:* "This house was designed to take the smallest part of the land, to catch the sun exactly right, to feed the eye with natural surfaces and unobstructed views of the valley. We love it."

2

On a 13-acre site near the newly established Cuyahoga Valley National Park, this carefully articulated house replaces a cabin the owners previously occupied on occasional summer weekends. The new structure, for a family with two daughters who now live at home, has been planned for a changing future. When new circumstances dictate, the present carport can be converted to a living room and the existing living room turned into a family room. Children's quarters are zoned away from parents' sleeping area and, because the owner often works at home, a private study has been provided upstairs in the rounded section.

The area immediately around the house is quite flat but the larger site is contoured and dips down to a stream. In establishing the pattern of openings, the architect tried to frame specific views, long and short, across the site—a device that helps establish an individual character for each interior space.

From concrete block foundations, the house springs up in lively somewhat angular massing. The construction is wood frame covered in 1- x 6-inch roughsawn cedar boards which were milled to form lap joints. The same cedar was used selectively inside where it was nailed directly to the studs. Other interior finishes include brick and gypsum board.

In order to retain the natural cedar color and character, a newly developed clear wood finish was applied to the exterior. If it performs as expected, no appreciable discoloration will occur as a result of weathering or natural aging.

The Erdos house, its massing nicely resolved, presents unexpectedly varied elevations from each successive point of the compass.

Architect: J. Lawrence Scott
 P.O. Box 151
 1822 Orchard Drive
 Bath, Ohio
Owner: Mrs. & Mrs. William Erdos
Contractor: William Erdos

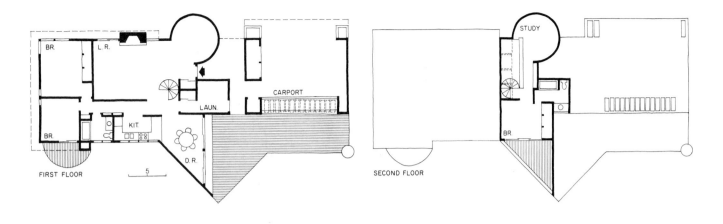

FIRST FLOOR   BR.   L.R.   LAUN.   CARPORT   KIT.   D.R.

5

SECOND FLOOR   STUDY   BR.

D. G. Olshavsky

 Architect Earl Combs has designed an unusual vacation house for a young family in a resort community on Long Island's South Shore. The program is hardly extraordinary but Combs has used rounded forms and symmetrical planning in ways that generate exciting spaces without producing either the inflexibility or the tormented functions that special shapes often produce.

Joseph Molitor photos

The strong circular forms of the Koplik house anchor it firmly to its site, a flat, sandy 100- by 164-foot property on Long Island's South Shore. Directly across the approach road stands a tall water tower. Combs sited the house on the diagonal to avoid opening its views squarely on the tower and, in laying out the plan, the architect also strove to preserve the mask of trees that gives the house a sense of seclusion.

The paired, elongated drums (photo above), clad in vertical cedar siding, are the most conspicuous element in its massing, but the heart of the house is the double-height volume in between (see plan). Here, under a central skylight, is the space to which all the others are keyed, a living room with a built-in, circu-lar seating element facing the deck and a view through a glass wall. Flanking this space on the lower level are kitchen, dining room, maid's room, den and stair. On the level above, over-looking the living room, are three bedrooms and two baths. A bridge links the two halves of the upper level.

The curved ends of the structure have 6 ft-4 in. radii and are built using sill plates cut from 2 x 12s and fitted together to form the arc. Plywood sheathing was then nailed to wood studs and finished in cedar.

Cedar siding is also the primary finish ma-terial for walls and partitions. Floors are oak strip with polyurethane applied. The ceiling structure is exposed. Lighting is either flush-mounted or recessed incandescent throughout the house. The glazing is accomplished using stock window and door assemblies and, when these occur in rounded planes, the variable depth of the reveals seems to emphasize the roundness of the forms.

The house has some 1900 square feet of enclosed space and extends outward with decks and walks in three directions. The treat-ment of these outside spaces, though strongly geometric, seems unforced and gracious—a happy transition between the naturalness of the site and the vigorously ordered forms of the house itself.

KOPLIK RESIDENCE, Long Island, New York. Owner: *Mr. and Mrs. Michael Koplik.* Architect: *Earl Burns Combs.* Contractor: *Steven Molzon.*

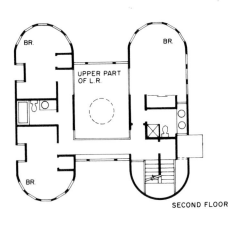

UPPER PART OF L.R.

BR.

BR.

BR.

SECOND FLOOR

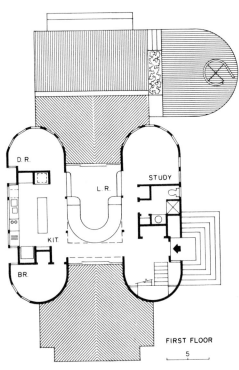

D.R.

STUDY

L.R.

KIT.

BR.

FIRST FLOOR

5

In the solid-void-solid scheme that Combs has selected for his massing, the reader might anticipate an entrance across the deck and into the central void along the axis of symmetry. Instead, Combs has created a more direct and interesting side entry (see plan above) that brings the visitor past the stair and into the central space from the back.

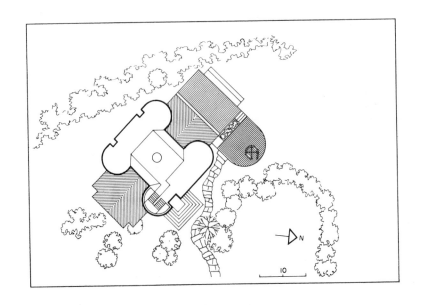

N

10

The den (above) and the entry-way and stair (below) are both spaces developed in the building's circular ends. The kitchen is located along an outside wall, notched for side light at the end of the counter. Bar seating provides an alternative to a more formal dining space beyond.

4

The important use of curved shapes in this house is to make it as abstract as possible—although in fact it is a simple, 14- by 70-foot winterized weekend and vacation house on the prairie in northwestern Illinois built within a $35,000 budget.

The important design idea is that the house is not four-sided, but two-sided—an idea established by the rounded ends divided by a louvered vertical strip on the centerline. And beyond that, the house is intended to be a series of oppositions or inversions. On the side facing the road (bottom in drawing, upper photo) the house is totally opaque and solid, with even the front door let in with curved shapes. Tigerman sees this side of the house as a performer on a stage, or as a proscenium, with an audience of apple trees to be planted 30 feet on center. The approach is deliberately not on axis—one is intended to see the house, then have it hidden behind the trees, enter the drive, "lose focus," and then unexpectedly come upon the house with no opportunity to study it or even know how big it is. Even its cedar wall

is "an opposition" to the natural trees planted in a geometric (un-natural) way.

Once you enter the house and move to the living spaces, you are immediately "thrust out of it"—with glass walls in an (unnatural) Mondrian pattern overlooking a section of the site that slopes down to a swimming pond and huge old trees beyond.

Functionally, the glass wall reflects the simple plan behind: The tall window lights the stair well, the small window adjacent is over the tub, the larger windows open to bedrooms on the upper level, dining and living spaces below. Guests sleep on curved built-in couches on the main level.

The Hot Dog House (as it is inevitably known) has 1,600 square feet of living space, for a cost of $22 per square foot.

PRIVATE RESIDENCE, northwestern Illinois. Architects: *Stanley Tigerman & Associates.* Contractor: *Donald Zimmerman.*

Philip Turner photos

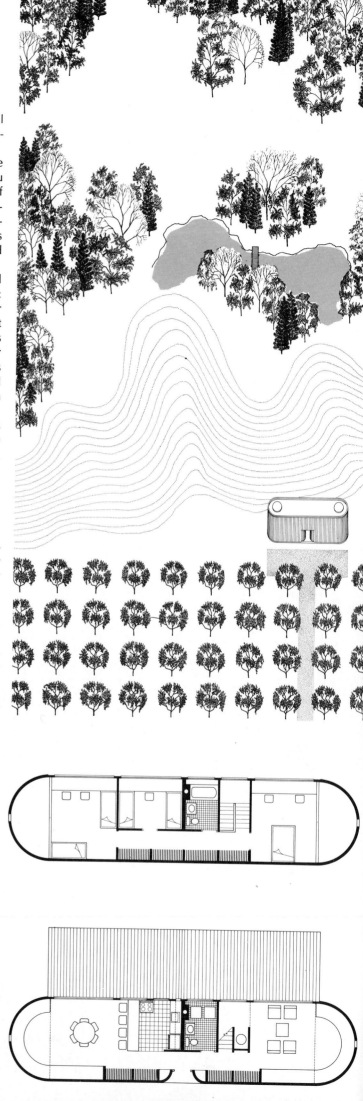

5

"To me, the marsh is a microcosm of life itself, constantly in a state of flux, never static, changing with the seasons, the days, with the tides, with the constant procession of wildlife—ducks, herons, hawks, shorebirds all feeding on what the tide brings in or, in ebbing, uncovers. . . ." Thus architect/owner Peter Woerner de-

scribes his view—a 90-acre tidal marsh facing Long Island Sound. The actual site is a long granite ridge at the edge of the marsh, a ridge that steps down to the eastward suggesting a natural series of half levels. Here, behind a scrim of hickory and oak, Woerner sited his house, a house he envisioned as springing from, and then returning to, the earth in a pure form—an easy and effortless arc.

On the uppermost level, under the arching roof form, the owner has a master bedroom, dressing room, bath and private deck overlooking the marsh. The

level below is given over to guest bedrooms and a studio that are separated by half a level. The lowest levels are kitchen, dining and living spaces, the dining space being framed in greenhouse sections (photo overleaf) and opening to a southern exposure. The architect reports that the greenhouse provides a passive solar heating situation with the brick floor over the ledge serving as a heat sink. The living room, drawn back from the glass wall, is sheltering and intimate.

The main perimeter arches were laminated from 2 by 12

planks of Douglas fir with a ½-inch thickness of plywood sandwiched in between. All joints are scarfed and staggered. Joists span between the arches and the whole structure is covered with ½-inch thickness of plywood which acts as a vast stressed skin.

Architect, engineer, owner, contractor:
  Peter Kurt Woerner
  182 Leetes Island Road
  Guilford, Connecticut
Location: Guilford, Connecticut
Graphics consultant: Christina Beebe
Photographer: Robert Perron

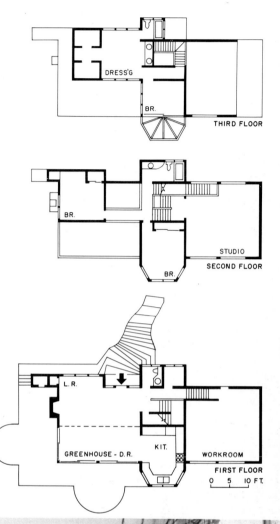

THIRD FLOOR

DRESS'G

BR.

STUDIO

SECOND FLOOR

BR.

BR.

L. R.

GREENHOUSE - D.R.

KIT.

WORKROOM

FIRST FLOOR

0   5   10 FT.

All the principal spaces in the Woerner house open through large expanses of glass to views of the marsh. The studio, photo above, is glazed using a standard industrial sash cut at its edges to fit the curvature of the roof. The plans show a simple, compact, well organized space.

The 45-degree angle: Another strong generator of exciting shapes

In the last dozen years, architects discovered the 45-degree angle (the 60-degree angle was used in many of Frank Lloyd Wright's house designs). As if to make up for all the years of not using it, for some years an extraordinary percentage of the houses by very good architects made strong use of this "new shape"—in plan, in elevation, and sometimes, as in the house that begins this chapter, as the total house form.

It's easy to see why: the forms, inside and out, that are generated, are exciting. They can create great sense of space in rooms, let in light from surprising angles, create everywhere a sense of surprise and the unexpected, and just plain look good.

Sometimes the use of the 45-degree angle as a "form-generator" is purely arbitrary—and that's all right. But often a rationale is clear—like the shape of the site, the desire to focus on a broad major view, or the desire to create some excitement on a featureless site. At any rate, in the houses that follow, you shall see . . .

The house by William Kessler uses triangular shapes not just to relate to the view, but to sidestep a beautiful grove of trees (page 132).

The house by Kirby Fitzpatrick uses a triangular shape to create one great (though informal) space in a tiny house (page 136).

In the Connecticut house by architect Len Perfido, the 45-degree shape is used to create rooms of extraordinary vitality and to create unexpected vertical spaces. Here, the angle only "peaks out" from place to place on the exterior (page 138).

In the house by Tasso Katselas, the 45-degree angle is used in plan at much smaller scale. Though the house itself is L-shaped, the angle is used to create small changes of direction in the walls; to create bay-window forms; and in a few strategic spots, to create stunning skylights by "lopping off" corner (see page 142).

A similar, if somewhat subdued use of the angle is made in Don Chapell's design for his own house (page 144), although the two houses are very different in form and formality.

The next three houses—by Alfred De Vido, Louis Sauer, and Norman Jaffe—use the angle in elevation in extremely strong roof shapes that give the houses strength and a sense of sculpture and drama (inside and out) on essentially featureless land.

The house by architect Thomas Larson (page 154) explores angular shape about as far as you can go. It is indeed "somewhat willful in character" but it clearly meets the clients' wishes for a house that is "spatially exciting and individualistic . . . for a couple that share with the architect a happy unconcern for self-conscious design . . ."

And the house by William Morgan *is* as far as you can go. It is a pyramid.

BOLD TRIANGLE DESIGN FOR AN ISLAND HOME

Architect Eliot Noyes studied this site near Mystic, Connecticut, followed his penchant for strong simple-shaped houses, and chose his design: a triangle. This two-level, dark-cedar-clad home that resulted setting on a rocky peak of a shoreline island, is distinctive, even ingenious, from whatever angle it's viewed. (From the air, it looks like a giant arrow directing pilots to an airport five miles away.)

The 180-degree view of scenic Ram Point Cove that the owners, The Reverend and Mrs. Francis Johnson, are able to enjoy is owed partly to a triangular screened porch adjoining the glazed living area and turned northwest toward the water.

In zoning the house, Noyes used the long, entry side for bedrooms, baths and kitchen, adding floor-to-ceiling windows to the bedrooms to draw in the southern sunlight.

Beyond this row of rooms is the large living/recreation area, including living room, dining and music areas. Broken up only by a freestanding stone fireplace, the room has direct access to the porch and the view through sliding glass doors.

In using the triangular shape, Noyes also took to task a problem

Norman McGrath photos

site. Not only was it small (less than half an acre), it was interrupted down the center by a large, rocky ridge. Noyes decided to build a lower level with an irregular, zigzag outline, and to "rest" a triangular second story on top to minimize removal of the rock.

The Johnsons, near retirement, didn't need much room for children, as most of theirs are grown, but their hobbies and favorite activities required ample work and storage space. In their previous Colonial-style house they were used to giving large dinner parties and wanted to do the same here. Their activities—boating, gardening, dogs—had an even better chance for development in this new location.

The entire lower level was designed with these outside interests in mind. Centered on a large entry room, it houses a workshop, bicycle room, boat storage room, carport and dog bath.

A utility-sewing room for Mrs. Johnson juts off the front of this level. From its windows she can get a clear view of approaching visitors as she works; its roof is a sun deck for the second story that opens off one of the bedrooms above.

In addition to a stairway, a small elevator up to the kitchen eases

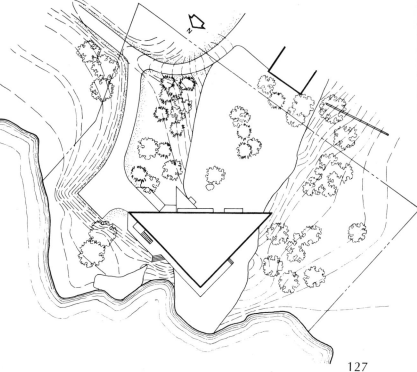

127

garbage and grocery hauling for the Johnsons. A skylight at the top of the stairs is one of many throughout the house—in the bedrooms, baths and kitchen. If these could be considered energy-savers, the lighting system over the large living area is a small-scale luxury. It is a vast grid of downlight fixtures, set four feet on center, with dimmers and group circuits. Almost any combination of lighting is thus possible to suit a variety of moods or times of day, and furniture can be shifted around more flexibly.

To fill one of the acute angles created by the house's shape, Noyes designed a breakfast nook off the kitchen. A small greenhouse outside the master bedroom, bluestone floor covering on the first level, and slate counters in the kitchen are other special features.

The house has a steel-frame structure with standard wood joists, on a concrete foundation, and is centrally air-conditioned.

RESIDENCE FOR THE REVEREND AND MRS. FRANCIS JOHNSON, near Mystic, Connecticut. Architects: *Eliot Noyes & Associates.* Engineers: *Arne Thune* (structural), *Peter Szilagyi & Associates* (mechanical/electrical). Lighting consultants: *Sylvan R. Shemitz and Associates.* Contractor: *Ole P. Jensen.*

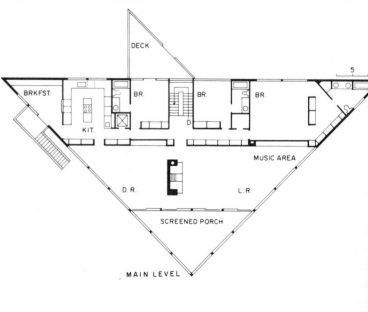

DECK

BRKFST.

KIT.

BR.

BR.

BR.

MUSIC AREA

D.R.

L.R.

SCREENED PORCH

MAIN LEVEL

5

Stairway (left), facing south, leads to elegantly furnished second floor, the main living area of the house. Glazed skylights like the one above, and full-length windows such as those in the master bedroom (below left) draw in energy-saving sunlight throughout the house. In the dining room, the Johnsons and their guests can overlook a scenic view of the cove, as they can in varying degrees from windows in the entire living area.

2

Lake Huron is the all-absorbing focus of this house, which is sited on a six-acre parcel on the lake's western shore. A grove of cedar trees, estimated to be over 100 years old, dominates the site. The usable building area between the trees fell naturally into a series of triangular clearings (aerial photo, below) and this, combined with the owner's request for privacy between the spaces, led to the plan of separate triangular units all fed from a central spine.

If, at first glance, the plan seems strained, on closer inspection its logic is apparent. Living, dining, kitchen and master bedroom spaces face the lake in the two easternmost pavilions. Behind these, but still opening on the diagonals toward the lake, are additional bedrooms and a caretaker's unit. The final pavilion, shown in the photos (but not in plan) is a garage and turned away from the lake view. Secondary spaces are carefully placed within these pavilions to augment their internal privacy.

There was no blunting of the traditionally troublesome acute angles. Kessler brought the glazing right to the wood wall and, in effect, "planted out" the corner. This was easily accomplished because each triangular pavilion is constructed over a concrete pedestal and slab.

Each section of the house has its own heating and cooling system. Standing water from the flat roofs is drained to a storm basin and then pumped to two remote dry wells. Domestic water is supplied from an on-site shallow well using submersible pumps.

The triangular geometry is skillfully elaborated inside in changes of level, in the edges on the dropped ceilings, and in the design of built-ins—all of which shape and enrich the spaces to which they are integral.

Architects: William Kessler
  and Associates, Inc.
  733 St. Antoine
  Detroit, Michigan
Owner: Mr. and Mrs. Warren J. Coville
Location: Lakeport, Michigan
Engineers: McClurg Associates (structural)
  Sanctorum & Associates (mechanical)
  Harry Hoffman (electrical)
Contractor: John Keils
Photographer: Balthazar Korab

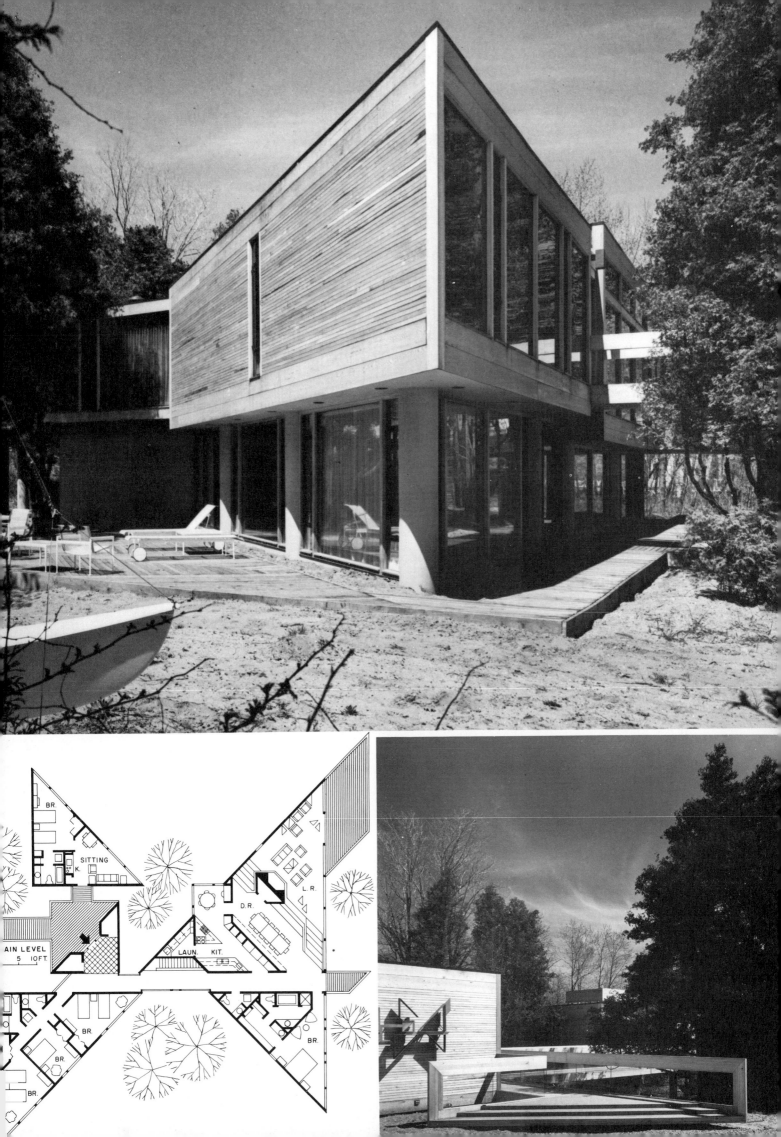

MAIN LEVEL
5 10FT.

BR.

SITTING
K.

L.R.

D.R.

LAUN. KIT.

BR.

BR.

BR.

BR.

COVILLE HOUSE
BY WILLIAM KESSLER
AND ASSOCIATES

The principal finish materials are cedar siding, drywall, carpet, travertine marble, ceramic tile and bronze glass, which are used in generous amounts. The detailing of these materials, as in the carpet (photo left), is designed to reinforce the triangular vocabulary of the house.

3

About 60 miles north of San Francisco, near the Napa Valley town of St. Helena, this weekend house, of about 1,700 square feet, is set into a hilltop clearing beneath towering pines.

Now and again, one can hear cones and branches fall onto the contour-clutching hip roof, laid up in red cedar shingles, pitching high over good-sized living, entertainment, and sleeping areas.

Because of the slope, the structure steps down, with two levels. At the entranceway, at the end of a mile-long drive, the second level, containing a guest room, protrudes over the front door and, to assure privacy, no other openings are placed on this side of the house. The lower-level living spaces, which the guest room overlooks, are expansive, opening out to the surroundings, and embellished with examples of Bay Area art. In a spatial free-for-all, the living room flows into an affable, kitchen-eating area and, just adjacent, the owner's study.

The planes of resawn, knotty cedar, used outside as well, and the overhead beams of fir, set up a unifying play of surfaces that is anchored in place by a hearth of Feather River travertine (browns, tans) from way up in the Sierras. Sunlight and moonlight take turns with the skylight above the hearth, the room being luminous even after dark when, most usually, beasts can be heard going bump in the night round about the terraces, laid down in local fieldstone and bordered with ferns.

Things going bump in the night are what the design is meant to fend off. Which is why the open sides of the house can be closed in, burglarproof, with big rolling "barn doors" that bolt into the concrete aggregate slab.

Like life in these parts, this house has a well-organized nonchalance; its elements work and play, as its occupants do, with no thought as to which is which.

Architect: Kirby Ward Fitzpatrick
447 Sutter Street
San Francisco, California
Private residence
Location: St. Helena, California
Landscape architect: Jonathan Herr
Contractor: H.S. Meinberger and Son
Photographer: Jim Ball

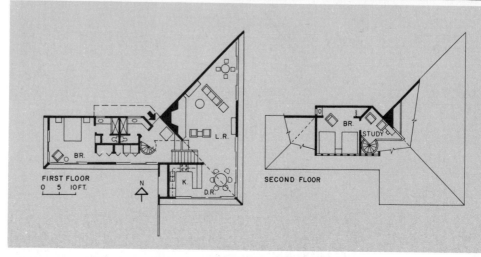

FIRST FLOOR
0 5 10 FT.
N
BR.
L.R.
K
D.R.

SECOND FLOOR
BR.
STUDY

4

This is a wonderfully complex house full of spaces that are complex in shape, opened by surprising changes in ceiling height, and lit by windows in unexpected places. The strong diagonal planes were arranged to create varied outdoor spaces—some sunny, some shaded—open to the rocky and wooded site in Weston, Connecticut. Inside (see plan opposite and interior photos, next spread), the walls—all at a 45-degree angle—create rooms that are unconventional in shape but, upon study, prove to be not only fun but functional, within a plan organization that is well zoned and meets a difficult program. The house was built to accommodate a young couple both of whom work, their young son, a person who cares for the child, and three sons from a previous marriage who visit for a few weeks at a time during the year. On the ground level (see plans), is the young son's bedroom with large closets for toy storage and a built-in desk; and a room for his nurse which could in the future serve as a guest room. The upper level loft, open to the living room below and with tree-top views over a golf course, is the owners' work area, with a 20-foot built-in desk. A foldout sofa permits the space to double as a sleeping loft when the older sons visit.

The focus of the house is a large, irregularly shaped living-dining-library space which accommodates all of the social activities of the family. The kitchen is large, and—since both Mr. and Mrs. Gold are avid cooks—it has a large institutional range. The reading-sitting area in the main living space opens to the master bedroom suite.

The 2,900-square-foot house is finished inside and out with clear cedar.

Architect: Leonard P. Perfido
 6415 Howe Street
 Pittsburgh, Pennsylvania
Owners: Michael and Sirje Gold
Location: Weston, Connecticut
Structural engineers: Robert Silmann
 Associates
Contractor: Michael Sochacki
Photographer: Maris/Semel

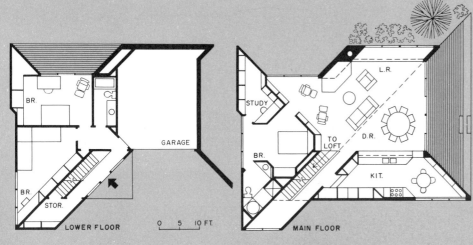

BR.

BR.

STOR.

GARAGE

LOWER FLOOR

0 5 10 FT.

STUDY

L.R.

BR.

TO LOFT

D.R.

KIT.

MAIN FLOOR

GOLD HOUSE BY LEONARD P. PERFIDO

The rooms of the Gold house by Leonard Perfido, shaped by strong diagonals, are irregular in shape and height. At left is the working area for the owners, which doubles as a sleeping loft when older sons visit. The other three views show how the dining area, main living space, and library-sitting area flow into each other. Space and light are borrowed in all directions . . .

5
The clients for this house have one child, a daughter in college. To give her the privacy and freedom she desires when she comes home to visit, they asked their architect, Tasso Katselas, to design for them two houses in one.

His triangulated plan (opposite page) includes a two-story element which contains a bedroom on the second floor and a small studio ten steps down. The daughter's quarters have their own private entrance from a terrace at grade. The studio window and entrance porch of the daughter's two-story suite can be seen to the left of the two-story living room in the photo above. Because of the sloping site, the house has three levels. The entrance, guest bedroom

and bath, the dining room and kitchen share the same elevation. The living room is three steps lower. The master bedroom, dressing room and bath share the top level with the daughters bedroom. The mezzanine overlooking the living room serves as a small office as does the cylindrical form at the intersection of the two wings.

At the bedroom level is a door which opens upon a bridge which spans the driveway and connects the house to a sundeck on the roof of the two car garage.

Architect Katselas had a completely free hand in the design of this house. His client is a fashion buyer for whom stylistic consistency is very important. He desired a totally designed house and left the ultimate

responsibility for furniture selection, tom designs, color and landscaping in hands of Katselas.

As is always true of good houses, th photographs do not do justice to the ex lence of the interiors. The living and dir spaces are lofty and elegant, yet not friendly. The custom cabinet work is es cially fine.

ROVIDA RESIDENCE, Elizabeth Towns Pennsylvania. Architect: *Tasso G. Katselas.* E neers: *R. M. Gensert Associates* (structu *James Sarver, P.E.* (mechanical); *Environmen corporated* (electrical). Consultants: *Paul Pla Design Associates* (interiors); *Joseph Hajnas sociates* (landscape). Contractor: *Century C struction Company.*

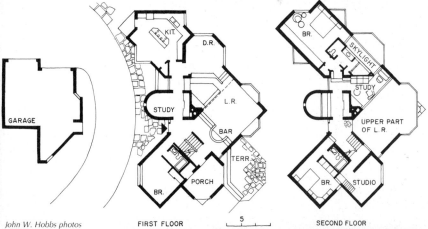

The plans are oriented to correspond with the photo above which indicates the two-car garage with its projecting wing, the bridge, the half cylinder at the entrance, and in the foreground the guest bedroom with the daughter's bedroom above it and her studio beyond. One of the most attractive parts of the house is the inglenook (below left), four steps below the dining room level. The plan provides several such appealing spaces.

GARAGE

KIT.

D.R.

STUDY

L.R.

BAR

TERR.

BR.

PORCH

BR.

SKYLIGHT

STUDY

UPPER PART OF L.R.

BR.

STUDIO

John W. Hobbs photos

FIRST FLOOR

5

SECOND FLOOR

/6

The tall pines with their characteristically abstract profiles were both an amenity and a starting point for the design of this year-round vacation house that architect Donald Chapell built for his own use. To retain as many trees as possible—and to keep them as close to the house as he could—Chapell had to generate an intricate, multifaceted plan shape and develop it carefully for privacy and view.

To an unusual degree, the house is a single large space with alcoves—alcoves that can be closed off when necessary by sliding doors. On the lower level, the living room, lined on two sides by glass, is flanked on the other two sides by kitchen and master bedroom. Two more sleeping spaces are located upstairs and are linked by a bridge over the living room—a bridge that also serves to shade the sitting area below from direct sunlight admitted through the large expanses of glazing to the south. Even larger openings occur on the north and provide a balanced, glareless daylight as well as views to the site.

The house is framed in wood stud and finished in cedar siding laid up vertically. The scale and texture thus created are welcome on the broad planar surfaces but do not interfere with the shifting patterns of shadow cast by the pines overhead. The same siding is used at various places inside for continuity and texture.

For summer comfort, the house is open and cross-ventilation is carefully provided. Windows are recessed not only to protect them from the sun but so that they can be left open during rainy weather without disturbing the regular air flow through the house.

The Chapell house is fun. It is spatially lively yet easy to maintain. The principal furnishing elements are built-in without sacrifice to flexibility and the house can be used and enjoyed by owner and occupants in a variety of ways.

Architect and owner:
Don Chapell
24 East 73rd Street
New York City
Contractor: John Caramagna
Photographer: Bernard Askienazy

Strings of red light bulbs (visible in the uppermost of the three small photos at left) are part of a larger lighting sequence that gives the interiors a warm rose glow during the evening. From outside on the deck, they make long, linear patterns that suggest, to the architect-owner, images of airport runways at night.

/7

The Bross residence, in East Hampton, is a compact solution to the problem of providing living spaces for a family of four on a one-acre site. The plan reveals a house tightly organized around a brick core which serves physically and spiritually as the center of the house. By turning the tall chimney breast off axis, De Vido underscored its symbolic importance and also eased the flow of space from entrance to living/dining area. This large central space is oriented toward a generous deck seen in the photo upper right.

The interior spaces strongly reflect the steeply pitched roofs and the vertical organization of space. Bedrooms, reached by a central, three run stair, are clustered on the second floor. The master bedroom overlooks the living room through a port fitted with a sliding door (see photo upper right). Above, on the uppermost level, is a small loft, open

to the stair, usable as a study, a studio or a small guest bedroom, depending on particular need.

The strong forms of this house and their graceful interplay give the Bross residence a compelling spatial character. As in several of the other houses in this group, the use of a single cladding material—cedar shingle (here stained dark)—serves to unify a complication of planes and projections. And overhead light sources, in the forms of skylight and clerestory, flood the interiors with natural light, giving them an especially welcome warmth and color enrichment at all seasons of the year.

BROSS RESIDENCE, East Hampton, New York. Architect: *Alfred De Vido*. Contractor: *Walter King*.

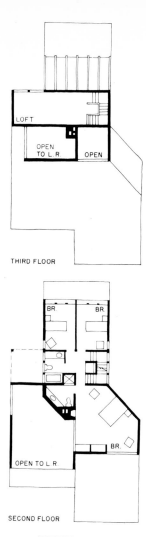

THIRD FLOOR

SECOND FLOOR

OPEN TO L.R.

FIRST FLOOR

5

N

The complex volumes of this house are clad in gray cedar and outlined by bright, orange-painted, metal fascias, downspouts and gutters. In the fireplace wall (photo below) between living room and study are several of many see-throughs. The area above the shoulders of the fireplace is open. The fire, the adjacent bar (left) and the TV, which swivels in a two-way nook (right), can be enjoyed from either room. A surprise interior window faces the flue.

Bill Maris photos, courtesy of House and Garden

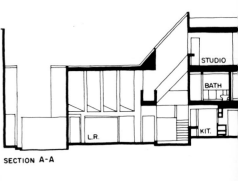

SECTION A-A

STUDIO

BATH

L.R.

KIT.

This house has all the major attributes of a vacation house—plenty of light, pleasant views, closeness to nature, and privacy—although it is on a confined 65- by 62-foot lot within a crowded shore community.

It is very near the sea, two doors away, but has no direct access to it. Nevertheless, architect Louis Sauer has ingeniously captured views of the sea from the roof deck above the third-floor studio, from the studio through the skylight and from the second-story bridge through the living room windows (see section opposite). With no other way of relating to the sea and no desirable views into the neighborhood, the house turns toward the sky and inward, providing its own environment.

Its focus is the central, three-story-high, skylighted atrium (see plans) with a fish pond under the main stair and a bed of tropical plants under the skylight. At the second-story level the atrium is crossed by two bridges, one to the master bedroom, the other connecting the main stair and the children's rooms. From the latter bridge to the studio is a flying stair which, like the other stairs, has open risers. These elements, visually exciting themselves, form a network of viewing platforms. The main bridge overlooks the two-story living room (photo lower left, opposite). The only rooms which are isolated from the atrium are some bedrooms. The kitchen looks right into it over the snack bar (center photo opposite).

The large, second-story living room windows (photos above and opposite) have angled fins that deflect direct afternoon sun and block the view of houses from the bridge so only the sea and sky are visible. Beneath them is another private landscape—an indoor planter for tropical plants within a fenced outdoor garden of native plants. Windows in the rest of the house are minimal and mostly placed in corners or light scoops for privacy.

The house has concrete block foundations, a wood frame structure, and cedar plywood siding. The pitched roof is lead painted orange.

SECOND FLOOR

FIRST FLOOR

Architects: LOUIS SAUER ASSOCIATES, 2011 Chancellor Street, Philadelphia, Pennsylvania
Project architect: Terence L. Brown. Project designer: Cecil Baker
Owner: Mr. and Mrs. Leonard Frankel. Location: Margate, New Jersey
Mechanical engineer: Williams Eads of M. Michael Garber Associates
Structural engineer: Joseph Hoffmann; Landscape architects: Collins and Dutot Associates
Interior design: Susan Frankel Maxman; Contractor: E. J. Frankel Enterprises, Inc.

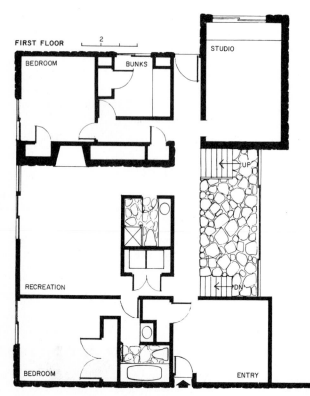

FIRST FLOOR

BEDROOM   BUNKS   STUDIO

UP

RECREATION

DN

BEDROOM   ENTRY

STORAGE

With characteristic candor, Norman Jaffe say that his design imagination draws freely fror the jumbled and unsorted after-images hundreds of buildings, old and new, that ove the years have printed themselves by reflex o his memory. During the design of this Lon Island house for film director Harold Becke one such graphic fragment intruded itself agai and again. It was Jaffe's fragile recollection an abandoned stone farmhouse, one of its gabl ends partially collapsed, that he saw on an Irisl meadow years ago. This picturesque image un doubtedly influenced the form of the Becke house, but it was the owner's instruction—"es tablish a connection with nature and don' break it"—that triggered the recollection an most influenced the choice of materials and th spirit of the detailing.

The plan is uncomplicated and largel self-explanatory. The only unusual element are a studio/screening room on the ground floor, a small multi–purpose loft reached by stair from the master bedroom suite and a outside closet where combustible film material can be stored at a safe remove from the house

The main structure is framed in massiv spruce timbers joined by gargantuan splic plates. The load-bearing masonry walls are laid

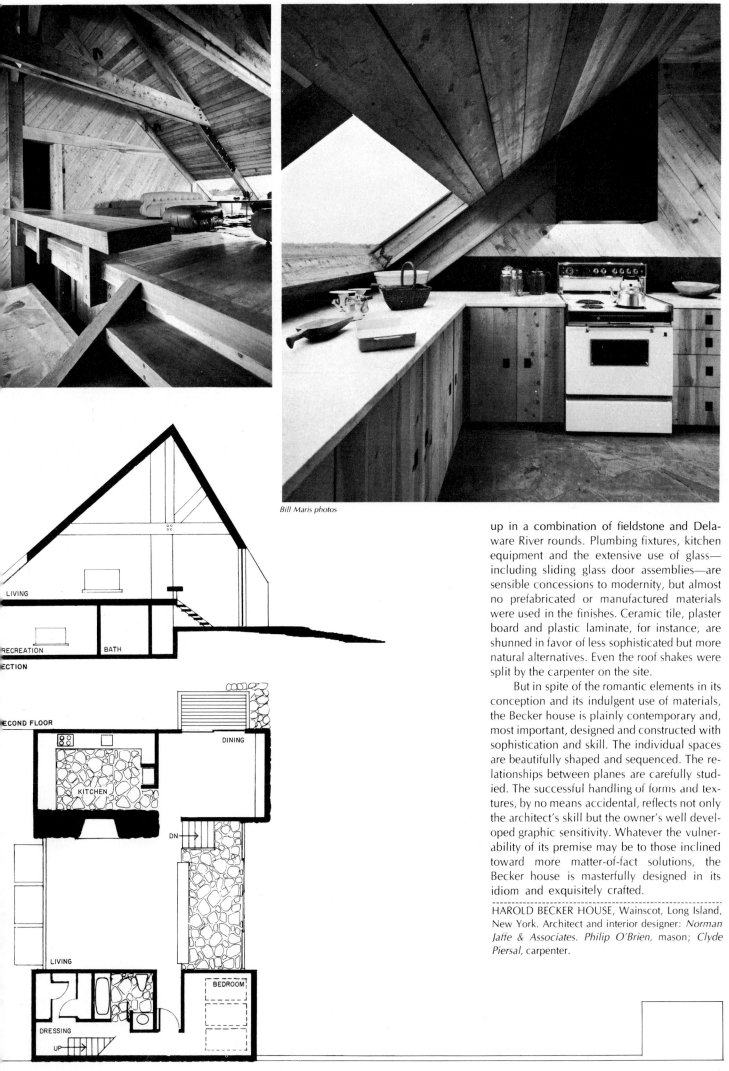

Bill Maris photos

up in a combination of fieldstone and Delaware River rounds. Plumbing fixtures, kitchen equipment and the extensive use of glass—including sliding glass door assemblies—are sensible concessions to modernity, but almost no prefabricated or manufactured materials were used in the finishes. Ceramic tile, plaster board and plastic laminate, for instance, are shunned in favor of less sophisticated but more natural alternatives. Even the roof shakes were split by the carpenter on the site.

But in spite of the romantic elements in its conception and its indulgent use of materials, the Becker house is plainly contemporary and, most important, designed and constructed with sophistication and skill. The individual spaces are beautifully shaped and sequenced. The relationships between planes are carefully studied. The successful handling of forms and textures, by no means accidental, reflects not only the architect's skill but the owner's well developed graphic sensitivity. Whatever the vulnerability of its premise may be to those inclined toward more matter-of-fact solutions, the Becker house is masterfully designed in its idiom and exquisitely crafted.

HAROLD BECKER HOUSE, Wainscot, Long Island, New York. Architect and interior designer: *Norman Jaffe & Associates. Philip O'Brien,* mason; *Clyde Piersal,* carpenter.

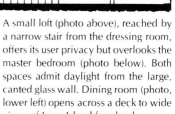

SECTION

LOFT FLOOR

STUDY

DN

A small loft (photo above), reached by a narrow stair from the dressing room, offers its user privacy but overlooks the master bedroom (photo below). Both spaces admit daylight from the large, canted glass wall. Dining room (photo, lower left) opens across a deck to wide views of Long Island farmland.

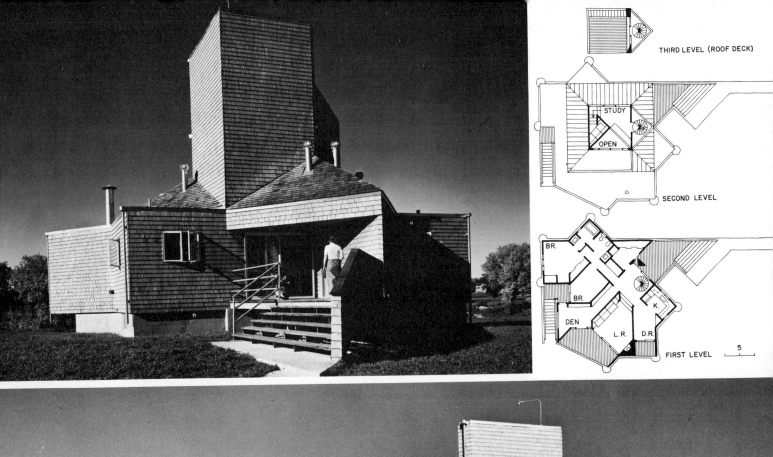

THIRD LEVEL (ROOF DECK)

SECOND LEVEL

STUDY

OPEN

FIRST LEVEL

BR.

BR.

DEN

K.

L.R.

D.R.

5

10

Rugged and angular in character, this small year-round house for a newspaper editor and his wife is located in Roseau, Minnesota, just below the Canadian border. The triangular site fronts on a stream and opens toward the west to unobstructed views of a golf course beyond. The owners, Mr. & Mrs. William Adams, wanted privacy—within and without—and stressed their desire for a house that was spatially exciting and individualistic.

Architect Thomas Larson developed internal privacy by careful zoning (see plan) and augmented this feeling through the use of level changes, small niches and a two-foot-high parapet in the living room. The plan contains two unusual components: a

private sun bathing platform on the roof and a mud room at the entrance—a practical necessity for climate control in a region where winter temperatures sometimes drop to 30 degrees below zero.

Framed in wood stud and sheathed in plywood, the Adams house is heated by forced air and insulated with double thickness of glass fiber batts. On wall and roof surfaces, the exterior finish material is red cedar shingle.

The unexpected complication of shapes give the plan a somewhat willful character, but the spaces seem to work well and flow together convincingly. The broken planes and angular development of the elevations aptly reflect the irregular interior

volumes. The interesting assortment of r vents, stove pipes, downspouts, rain leac and whip antenna gives the house a pl santly unedited appearance and sugg that architect and owners share a happy concern for self-conscious design as wel a firm grasp of the exigencies of builc and function.

ADAMS RESIDENCE, Roseau, Minnes Architect: *Thomas N. Larson—John Warren sistant.* Engineers: *Michael Jolliffe* (structu *Robert Fairbanks* (mechanical). Contra *Arthur Anderson.*

154

SECTION

Interior finish materials are cedar boards for ceilings, plasterboard for partitions and carpeting or sheet vinyl on all floors. Counters are covered in plastic laminate. Foundation walls are concrete block.

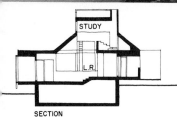

SECTION

Phokion Karas photos

11

This earthform house in central Florida is built into the crest of a hill that overlooks citrus groves on the valley floor 230 feet below. From its uppermost level, tucked under a hipped roof, the owner can look out in every direction across enormous expanses of view that reach into five surrounding counties. The architect reports that on one occasion from this vantage he was able to count seven separate thunderstorms in progress simultaneously.

In sharp contrast, views from the lower level are confined and intimate. The ends of the cruciform plan open through glass doors to small partially-enclosed courts (photo above) which, by their different orientation, architectural treatment and planting, provide a variety of sensory experience.

The structure is reinforced concrete block with tie beams, pilasters and a concrete slab poured in place. All exterior walls are earth-insulated except where glazing occurs. Partitions are plaster board on wood stud, glass is solar gray tinted, and the roof is finished in clay tile.

The original elevation of the hilltop was just about the level of the first floor slab. The pyramidal flanks of the building, therefore, represent an extension of the hill inclined upward at about 18 degrees.

In addition to being a graceful and interesting solution for this exposed but isolated hilltop site, the parti is reminiscent of earth mound buildings developed centuries ago by the various Indian tribes that inhabited central Florida before its present settlement. Reinterpreted here, the earthform idea seems just as compelling today.

Architect: William Morgan
    project architect: Thomas A. McCrary
    220 East Forsyth Street
    Jacksonville, Florida
Private residence
Location: Central Florida
Engineers:
    Haley Keister (structural)
    Roy Turknett (mechanical)
Contractor: Howard Woodward
Photographer: Creative Photographic Svc.

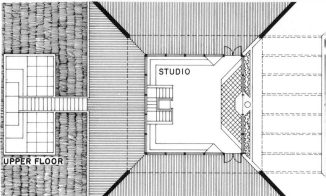

STUDIO

UPPER FLOOR

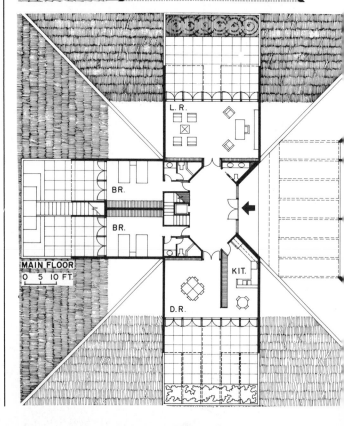

L. R.

BR.

BR.

D. R.

K I T.

MAIN FLOOR
0   5   10 FT.

Sometimes the form of a house grows sort of inevitably from its materials (some houses that had to be masonry or metal)

Architect Eliot Noyes' design for a Connecticut house (overleaf) *is* two stone walls—they dominate the site, the exterior of the house, and all of the rooms

Architect Don Singer's design for a concrete-block house (page 162) makes wonderfully straightforward use of that wonderfully straightforward building material; yet it is in no way simple—but indeed, rather sculptural.

A much more sophisticated house (page 164, by Terry Twitchell and Nancy Maio) makes use of a much more sophisticated block; the blocks have a rough, marble-chip aggregate exposed. This house, too, makes clear the unfairness of linking any material to a particular kind of use—for there is nothing of the "warehouse" or "industrial look" to this very grand house.

In their design for a house in Illinois (page 168), architects Booth and Nagle have created a strong and surprising house from that most solid and staid of materials—brick.

The two final houses in this chapter are the most unusual:

Architect Frank Gehry's house for an artist is unusual in many ways: none of its walls are parallel, its roof is skewed, the partitions are changeable—all to create spatial illusions, changing relationships, constantly changing moods. In such an abstract composition, the use of corrugated, galvanized metal seems singularly appropriate.

Finally, architect Barton Myers' design in steel does seem, as the copy describing the house suggests, to "blur the distinction between industrial and residential design vocabularies," and to "transfer the precise elegance of steel columns, metal deck, and the delicate tracery of open web joists from factory to home . . . easily and persuasively."

Intellectually, you know that these masonry and metal houses could have been built differently . . . but as you study them they seem just right the way they are.

The thrust of the house from its rocky perch is especially evident in the t
views from the valley, above: The photograph at left shows the study end
the gallery while the one above it shows the entrance. The cantilevered livi
room, far right, has a deck and is entered from the gallery, right, as
most other rooms.

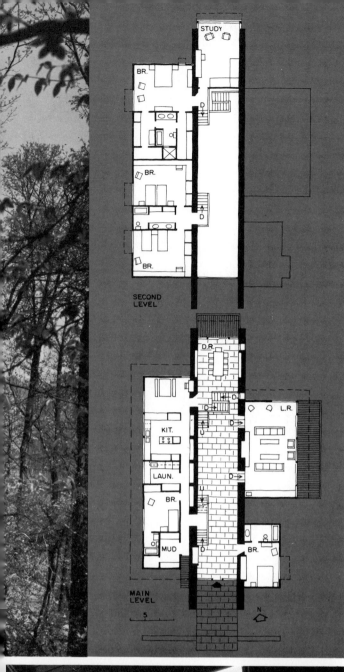

STUDY

BR.

BR.

BR.

SECOND LEVEL

D.R.

KIT.

LAUN.

BR.

MUD

L.R.

BR.

MAIN LEVEL

5

N

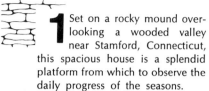

1 Set on a rocky mound overlooking a wooded valley near Stamford, Connecticut, this spacious house is a splendid platform from which to observe the daily progress of the seasons.

In order to minimize the difficulty of building upon the ledge rock, Eliot Noyes chose to build two massive, parallel stone-concrete walls from which the various rooms cantilever on post-tensioned concrete beams. The 14-foot wide central gallery, in which owner Robert Graham can display objets d'art from his New York City gallery is seen by Noyes as an indoor street. One moves through the stone walls into rooms as if he were entering separate houses from a narrow alley.

It is a scheme with which Noyes has experimented for a long time.

Thus the plan can be seen as a variation upon Noyes' own famous house: two separate houses across a garden wrapped by a stone wall. Here the garden (ivy has been planted in the crevices of the walls) is enclosed by the stone walls and the two houses are outside the enclosure. The gallery also serves as a lively ballroom when an orchestra plays from the study during parties.

The three-foot thick walls were built using three-foot high slip-forms which ran the entire length of the walls, 94 feet long. Heavy steel mesh, 8 inches in from each side of the form was wired to vertical steel rods. Selected rocks were pushed into place between the mesh and the form. Concrete was then poured from the center and allowed to seep out to the form through the stones. When the concrete had hardened, the forms were raised and the operation repeated.

Joseph W. Molitor photos

Architect: ELIOT NOYES
Eliot Noyes and Associates, 96 Main St., New Canaan, Conn.
Owner: Robert Graham, Jr.
Location: Fairfield County, Connecticut
Structural engineer: Viggo Bonnesen
Mechanical engineer: John L. Altieri
Landscape architect: Peter G. Rolland
Contractor: Sam Grasso Co., Inc.

2 The low-budget house on a 50- by-100 foot suburban lot is a problem which many architects have faced. But few have solved it as smoothly as Donald Singer has here. The building lot, slightly longer but no wider than the panel, opposite, in which the plan is placed, dictated the linear scheme which in turn allowed concrete block masonry to be used in a remarkably straightforward way. This is an unusual degree of architectural unity for a low price.

But unity in this case does not mean simple plan geometry. Three distinct volumes interlock at the entrance to produce lively spatial sequences, different views from each room, extreme privacy and minirnal circulation space. These virtues are achieved with construction economies that take into account the special problems of Florida building codes. Because of hurricanes, roof structures must be tied to a reinforced concrete beam at the top of all bearing walls which is itself directly connected to the footers (detail opposite, bottom). The nylon-asbestos roof surface also covers the fascias and eliminates possibility of roof-edge leakage completely.

Finally, the entire house is ti[e] together by a single air-conditic[n] ing duct. This spine (detail opp[o] site, bottom), requiring less th[an] 50 feet of supply duct, also p[ro] vides lowered ceilings in the pa[ss] ages which help define the din[ing] room and which emphasize [the] living room.

Architect: DONALD SINGER, 1301 S. E. 2nd Court, Fort Lauderdale, Florida
Owners: Mr. and Mrs. Joseph Schmidt
Location: Coconut Grove, Florida
Engineers: Houha and Harry Associates
Lighting consultant: Edison Price
Interior design: Dennis Jenkins
Contractor: Henry Roloff

SCREENED AREA

L.R.

A

D.R.

LAUN.

BR

BR

PLAY

N   5

Joseph W. Molitor photos

The living room (top right), dining room and master bedroom with enclosed garden (center), and children's playroom each have a different outdoor vista. Exterior views (opposite) emphasize the sculptural richness of house. Lettering on entrance continues inside, spells owner's name.

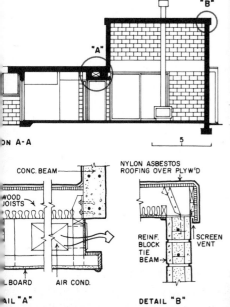

"B"

"A"

ON A-A   5

CONC. BEAM

NYLON ASBESTOS ROOFING OVER PLYW'D

WOOD JOISTS

REINF. BLOCK TIE BEAM

SCREEN VENT

L BOARD   AIR COND.

AIL "A"   DETAIL "B"

3 For a gently sloping, sparsely wooded, 2.5-acre site amid fine traditional houses in Harrison, New York the Architects Design Group created a house of extraordinary strength and assurance.

Its substantiality is produced by a clear-cut geometry, with solids dominating voids, and the use of a minimum number of materials. The square, with its stability as a form, is reiterated in the plan (overleaf), in some windows (photos opposite), in the opening around the front door (photo below), in the mantel and in the concrete blocks. And the blocks themselves, with exposed, marble-chip aggregate, contribute in thickness and texture as well as shape to the solidity the house conveys.

The high degree of geometrical order holds the separated parts of the house together. In plan it is composed of three square pavilions extending from three corners of the square, sunken forecourt and connected on one side by the stairwell and entry and on the other by the dining room and corridor. The two diagonals established by this arrangement are repeated in the scoring of the terrace paving which fills out another, larger square that ties the three pavilions together. The major diagonal is in line with the longest view towards which the living room, balcony study and terrace are oriented. The herringbone pattern of the oak floor also brings the diagonal into play.

Circular forms are used in areas of motion—the auto court, entry, stairwell and dog run—and to provide transitions between the undulating ground and rectilinear house.

Although the house gives a strong feeling of enclosure, reinforced by its masonry corners, it relates generously to the outdoors. All the major ground floor spaces have sliding glass doors onto the terraces.

Architects: TERRY G. TWITCHELL and NANCY A. MIAO of Architects Design Group (T. G. Twitchell, R. C. Abrahamson, V. Paukulis) 16 East 52nd Street, New York, New York
Location: Harrison, New York
Engineers: Joseph Biren (structural); Dalton & Dunne (mechanical)
Interior design: Andre Fiber
Contractor: Gilbert Merenda Construction Co.

By careful proportioning, the architects have established strong and deliberate contrasts between solids and voids and circular and square forms. They have also emphasized the rough concrete by playing it off against the metal canopy (right) and reflective glass.

James Brett photos

The entry (photo left) and living room (photo right) are grand, two-story spaces illuminated at the ground and upper levels. The Italian marble mantel in the living room is expressive of the geometry of the whole house. The clerestory topping the stair tower casts light into the well and balcony library (center photo) formed by shelves along the railing. The kitchen-breakfast area (bottom photo) has a corner exposure, like that of the living room, to the long view. As seen in the plan (below) the house is zoned into kitchen-service, living-study and sleeping wings. The children's and guest rooms upstairs can be closed off when not in use.

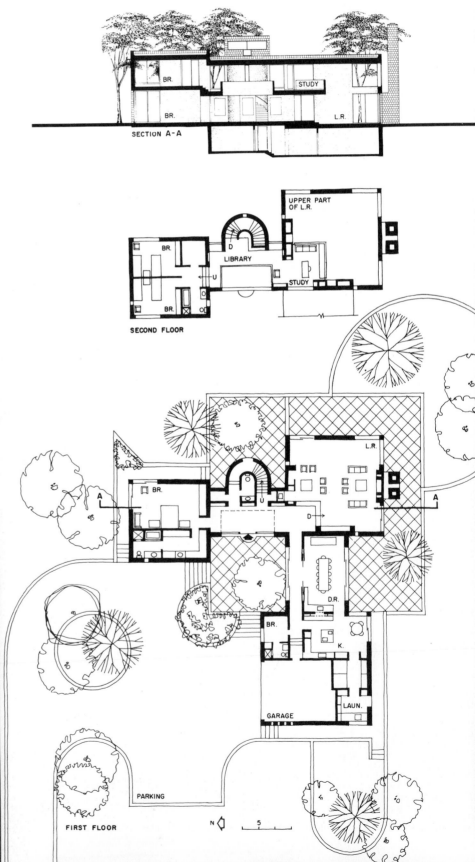

SECTION A-A

SECOND FLOOR

FIRST FLOOR

N   5

PARKING

4

Before this house was built for them on a suburban site in Hinsdale, Illinois, the owners lived in a large and elaborate mansion "with too many rooms and too much complication in general." Deciding to try to simplify their lives, they commissioned architects Booth & Nagle to design a house for them that was a cleaner statement of a more relaxed living style. Neighboring houses were in a neo-Georgian idiom, typically clad in brick and planned around a central entry and stair. The architects elected to adopt this theme but reinterpret it in a way that would be spatially liberating, easy to maintain, and, above all, fun to live in.

The approach to the Barr residence leads to a central entry hall with a living room opening to the left, a kitchen and dining space to the right. A circular stair at the end of the hall leads to bedrooms above. Much of the fun of the house—and its only complica-tion—grows out of the diagonal relationships developed by rotating certain of the elements through 45 degrees. The justification for the rotation, in addition to the spatial liveliness it creates, is to turn toward longer views that are not blocked by adjacent houses that flank in an orthagonal relationship on either side.

Large openings, including skylights, bring generous amounts of daylight deep into the house, printing white walls with shafts of sunlight and shadow in ever-changing patterns that reduce the need for wall decoration to an absolute minimum.

Moving around the house, inside or out, the planes unfold in an interesting progression revealing partial views to the second story and sometimes, through ribbons of plastic, the sky beyond.

Architects: Booth & Nagle
230 East Ohio Street
Chicago, Illinois
Owner: Mr. & Mrs. Warren Barr, Jr.
Location: Hinsdale, Illinois
Engineers:
Weisinger-Holland (structural)
Contractor: The Maddock
Construction Company
Photographer: Philip Turner

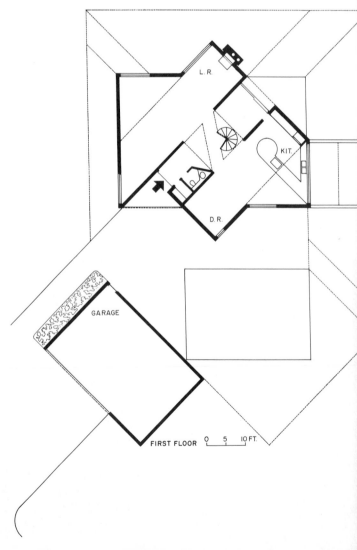

FIRST FLOOR 0 5 10 FT.

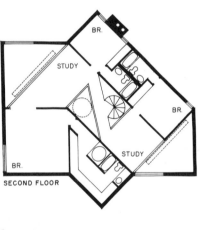

The exterior walls are face brick set in a colored mortar. Inside, the finishes are wood parquet for floors, ½-inch gypsum board on all partitions and ceilings. Colors are subdued, textures are kept in a fairly narrow range. Simplicity and ease of upkeep governed most of the detailing, especially at the great glass openings.

BR.

STUDY

BR.

BR.

STUDY

SECOND FLOOR

5

An unusual concept for a residence is Gehry's design for an artist, Ron Davis. A temporary combination of residence and studio (a separate studio is planned for later) is located on a three-and-one-half-acre site in Malibu with views to the south and west of the ocean and to the north and east of mountains. The objective of the architect was to create a minimal structure in which Davis could arrange space for his own special and changing needs. A trapezoidal form (reminiscent of the hay barn design) was developed from a close collabo-

ration between artist and architect, and relates strongly to Davis' paintings (mostly abstracts based on strong use of perspective).

From a 30-foot-high corner, the roof slants steeply to a 10-foot height at the opposite corner. Windows—in varying sizes and shapes (and reflective glass on the south wall)—and a large 20- by 20-foot centered skylight allow more than adequate natural light for the artist's work. These unconventional shapes add a new dimension and different perspective to each side of the house. The use of corrugated, galvanized metal on the exterior permitted an enlargement of the house's size to 5000 square

feet while keeping within the owner's budget.

The angular and high ceiling allows a flexibility in use of the space, including loft space, which could be expanded to a complete second floor within the structure, thus doubling the floor area. Openness for work area and display of art was achieved through the use of only three center columns and few partitions. To increase the flexibility for the artist, Gehry originally proposed that everything, including wall partitions, be on wheels, allowing spaces to be changed according to need and function. This was not done, but there are very few permanent partitions, none full ceiling height. A

Marvin Rand photos

UNDERFLOOR ACCESS SPACE

SECTION A-A

SKYLIGHT

partial second level (top, far right) was built to allow an unusual place to sit, talk, sketch or view art work.

One of Gehry's aims is to create spatial illusions. In designing for these he uses unusual shapes—and this design surely avoids the obvious and predictable. "If you move a chair or a wall," says Gehry, "you don't know what's going to happen to its relationships. Night brings another change. Like the sea, the moods are endless."

DAVIS RESIDENCE/STUDIO, Malibu, California. Architects: *Frank O. Gehry & Associates, Inc.—Frank O. Gehry; C. Gregory Walsh, Jr.,* design team. Structural engineer: *Joseph Kurily.* Contractor: *John Fernandez, of Jondol Company.*

6

There have been earlier attempts (few as successful) in Canada, the U.S. and elsewhere to blur the distinction between industrial and residential design vocabularies. Perhaps it was always a needless distinction, but it is still stimulating to see the steel columns, metal deck and the delicate tracery of open web joists transfer their precise elegance from factory to home so easily and persuasively. Inside the basic framework that these elements create is a secondary level of modification and texturing. It includes sculptured ductwork that traces powerful linear patterns throughout the house. It includes drop screens that temper the daylight at outside wall or skylight. And it also includes the entirely appropriate use of unexpected hardware and fixtures that are always within the residential designer's reach but seldom find their way into his specifications. It is a beautifully conceived house and even those whose cup of tea it is not will find much to linger over in its use of materials and its details.

The plan of the Wolf house is deceptively simple. It is a two-story, rectangular volume with a bite out of the center of one of its long sides—a bite which admits light and offers views from the normally "dead" waist section of such plans.

The house is lifted above the site to minimize the foundation problems that might otherwise have developed on 20 feet of new fill over a subterranean stream. The upper level contains bedrooms, baths, play area and study. Below, the principal spaces are arranged to take advantage of views to the park at the west. The closed side of the house, clad in aluminum siding, faces neighbors to the east.

In its rhythms, its textures and the handling of its details, the Wolf residence is beautifully organized and very skillfully executed.

Architect: Barton Myers
 formerly of
 A.J. Diamond & Barton Myers
 322 King Street
 Toronto, Ontario
Owners: Lawrence and Mary Wolf
Engineers:
 Read Jones Christoffersen, Ltd (structural)
 William Trow Assoc. Ltd. (foundations)
 G. Granek Assoc. Ltd. (mechanical)
Cost consultant: A.J. Vermeulen, Inc.
Contractor: Lawrence Wolf
Photographers:
 T. Kitajima of
 Y. Futagawa & Associates
 except as noted

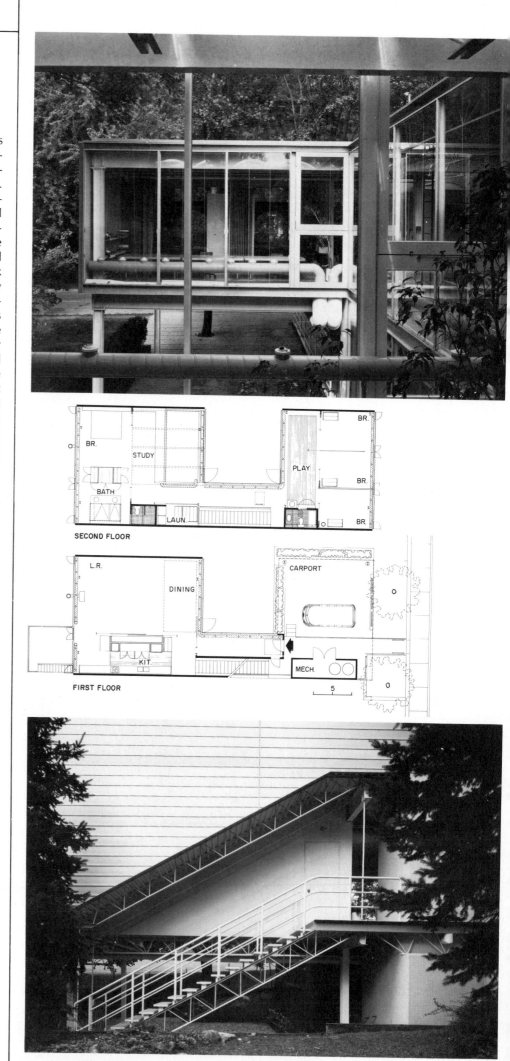

SECOND FLOOR

FIRST FLOOR

The owner's comment, in describing his vision of the house, is significant: "We saw the house as the ultimate new product, the mass market space and flexibility solution of the future."

A final word on the exceptions that prove the rule: Two romantic houses

As we've seen in the previous chapters, almost any house can be classified by its geometric roots. There are, after all, only so many basic geometric shapes. Like the houses in the first chapter, which have their roots in traditional forms; or those in the second, in which the design began with techniques of energy conservation; these last two houses—while they could be classified as being generated from geometrical forms—really resist such categorization. In the case of these houses, the design seems to have been drawn (only the architect knows for sure) from a combination of factors: from the site, from the views, from a bit of fantasy. To this editor, they are very romantic houses—and maybe that is good enough to justify this final chapter.

However, in the wonderful, wide-open world of deciding what makes a good house for you and your family, you can make up your own categories, your own rules, your own mind. And, with a little luck, live happily ever after . . .

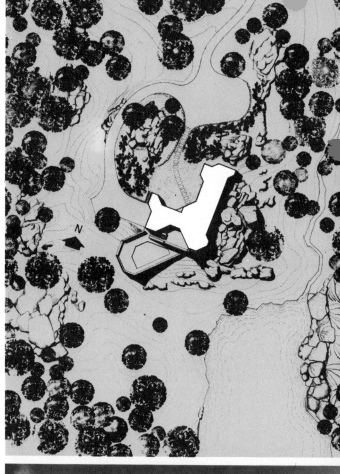

1 Designed to dramatize the virtues of an unexpected site —an old quarry gorge fed by a stream—this house leads the visitor from a quiet, one-story and almost symmetrical entrance court which shields the view, into rooms that open wide to rocks, quarry, pool and stream—and to a house that is as multi-faceted as the vistas.

In the program for the house, the architects note that, "the client for this house was a young couple with two small children. They wished the house to be informal, easy to maintain and geared to family living with no resident help. Their most important concern was a house allowing maximum enjoyment from their site, which they wanted to leave as natural as possible. They also wanted to have the principal rooms of the house filled with sunlight all day."

The architects have achieved all these objectives with considerable inventiveness. An L-shaped structure was devised to rim the edge of a relatively flat piece of high ground on the 22-acre site. A small-scale court and little lawn were created inside the "L," and closed on the other sides by natural rock formations, an earth mound and a raised flower-growing area. The rest of the site was left in its natural state.

To assure the desired sunlight and views, the basic L-shaped plan was faceted with many angles and fitted with big glass areas turned to focus on every possible vista.

Inside, the house is zoned into a bedroom wing, a kitchen-dining wing, and indoor/outdoor living areas which form the central hub of the plan. Both parents and children have small suites in the bedroom wing. The master bedroom is adjoined by a study/sitting room, and the children's area has two little bunk/study spaces flanking a living/play room. A guest room completes the bedroom wing. At the opposite end of the house is a dining room, and a big kitchen with a space for family meals. From the kitchen there is a view of the entrance court as well as a view across the upper deck to the living room and to the rock face of the quarry beyond. The big feature of the living room is a fireplace set between angled window walls to give views of everything all at once.

On the lower level of the house are garage and service spaces, and a playroom with access to the reinforced-concrete swimming pool and wood terrace on the same level.

In spite of its angularity, the house is simply framed as can be seen by the interior ceilings of exposed fir beams on a 24-inch module and 1-by-6 boarding (photos overleaf). The exterior is a cream-colored stucco, on wood frame on the upper floor and on concrete block below. The interiors have walls of painted gypsum board and floors of mottled green and purple slate or deep-pile brown carpet. The total interior effect is light, bright, airy—and gives the sense that spaces are larger than they really are.

Architects: KEITH KROEGER and LEONARD PERFIDO
Location: Residence in Waccabuc, New York
Mechanical engineer: George Langer
Structural engineer: Bob Silman
Landscape architects: Kroeger-Perfido
Interior design: Kroeger-Perfido
Contractor: Frank Calogero, A. Poccia & Sons

In strong contrast to the quiet facade of the entrance court (photo bottom right), the sides of the house which overlook the craggy rocks of the quarry gorge are intricate, faceted and very much in scale with the dramatic aspects of the site. On arriving at the house one cannot see the quarry until actually entering any of the major rooms.

Bill Maris photos

Architects Kroeger and Perfido have created a living room for this house that is, in effect, half indoors and half out, separated by a diagonal glass wall (photos below and right). The breakfast area has a corner chopped off in similar fashion for a little outdoor deck (bottom photo).

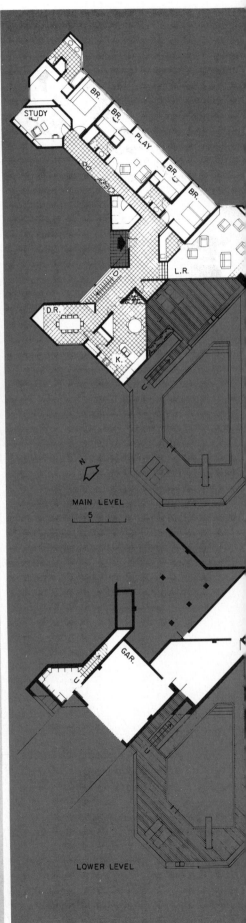

MAIN LEVEL

LOWER LEVEL

From higher up on the hill (photo opposite) where neighboring houses overlook it, the Lieto residence presents a carefully studied and articulated series of shed and pyramidal roof forms. This high degree of particularization expands the house visually and suggests—but only suggests—the spatial hierarchy within. Entry is from the downhill side. Stairs lead from the entrance up past the sunroom to the double-height living room under the largest of the three pyramidal roofs and then up four more steps to a den that doubles as a guest bedroom. The master bedroom, with dressing and bath complex, occupies the uppermost level. Thus the spatial development of the house is a series of interconnecting spaces that become more private as they step up the hillside. And only from the upper level is the entire volume of the house made visible and comprehensible.

The Lieto residence is a house of somewhat indeterminate scale owing chiefly to the wide range in the sizes of window and door openings. The windows were designed to frame specific views of the site, and most openings are tall and slender because the surrounding tree clusters are so vertical.

The hillside wraps partway around the house to form the beginnings of a topographic bowl into which the house is carefully set. There is a sense of partial enclosure by the site forms that creates an active relationship between house and setting. Decks project on three elevations to anchor the whole composition.

The over-all image is slightly Romantic—but if it owes something in its materials and its picturesque massing to the American Shingle Style, the debt is not great. The Lieto house develops logically from its own design assumptions—assumptions like these: small things can be as complex as big things; neighbors do not want to look down on flat, built-up roofs; and historicism still has an important place in contemporary residential design.

Architects:
 Walter D. Brown and
 Lawrence R. Jacobs
 35 Mercer Street
 New York City
Owner:
 Mr. & Mrs. Edward Lieto
Contractor: Joseph Loria
Photographer: Lawrence D. Queen

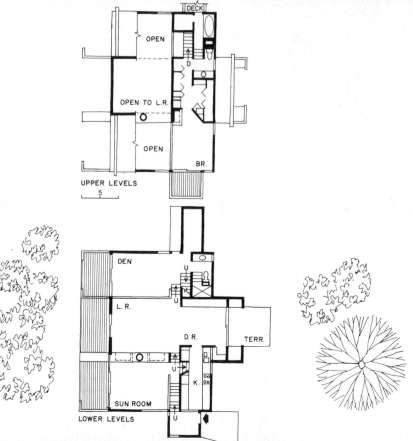

DECK

OPEN

OPEN TO L.R.

OPEN

BR.

UPPER LEVELS

5

DEN

L. R.

D. R.   TERR.

K.

SUN ROOM

LOWER LEVELS

The rooms are oriented to ensure maximum sunlight in the sun room (left, above) and an easterly view for the dining space. The den (left, below) can be closed off with an operable curtain that is hidden in a pocket when not needed.

Index